The Underdogs

William Weintraub
THE UNDERDOGS

McClelland and Stewart

The Canadian Publishers
McClelland & Stewart Limited
25 Hollinger Road,
Toronto M4B 3G2

Printed and bound in Canada

Canadian Cataloguing in Publication Data

Weintraub, William, 1926-
    The underdogs

ISBN 0-7710-9012-9

I. Title.

PS8545.E35U54   C813'.5'4   C78-001599-1
PR9199.3.W446U54

All the events and characters in
this book are fictitious. Any resemblance
to persons living or dead is
purely coincidental.

For Magda

Nationalism is an infantile disease. It is the measles of mankind.

Albert Einstein

1

In the Republic of Quebec, the entire month of June had been set aside to celebrate the twentieth anniversary of the founding of the state and its separation from the rest of Canada. The President called for revelry every night, and issued a proclamation declaring that during the month's span of thirty days there would be twenty-one public holidays.

At first, only modest festivities had been envisaged, in view of the country's bankrupt condition. But four months before the anniversary, the Soviet Union had come through with a large loan. At once the government decided to spend the money on the most lavish party ever held in the young republic. The Soviets had stipulated that the loan be used to repair crumbling factories and rickety railroads, but the leaders of Quebec considered these projects to be of much lower priority than the need to stimulate national pride.

The *Bureau de la fierté nationale* went to work on plans for the merrymaking. There would be parades, fireworks, and dancing in the streets. Visits would be paid by foreign heads of state. Thousands of costumed actors would appear in colossal pageants, depicting such historic events as the Fourth Referendum (June 24), the Proclamation of Sovereignty (June 25) and the Battle of Pointe Fortune (June 26).

In Montreal, blue-and-white bunting would flutter from every building. Statues of the Founding Fathers would be unveiled on the Boulevard du 15 Novembre, the elegant thoroughfare formerly known as Sherbrooke Street. Nearby, on the campus of the Université Maurice Duplessis, formerly McGill University, President Chartrand himself would open the Temple de la Langue Française, a new and magnificent structure built to apotheosize the official language of the state.

In the huge amphitheatre of the temple, poets, bards, and belletrists from many countries would attend a conference extolling the glory and the grandeur of the French language, which now reigned unquestionably supreme throughout the republic. For although a great many English-speaking people still lived in Quebec, the English language had no more status there than Swahili, Esperanto or Pig Latin.

* * *

"... *et les savants venant du Sénégal, Mali, Gabon et Haute Volta....*" As the commentator described the preparations for the Congress of the French Language, Paul Pritchard listened intently to the little transistor radio clipped to his belt. At the same time he walked slowly along the furrow, sowing his cauliflower seeds in the soft, black earth. "... *mettant la dernière main au temple magnifique....*" What idiocy, thought Paul. What the country needed was a modern fertilizer plant, not this monstrous temple, which would cost millions and serve no practical purpose.

By now he had come to the end of the last cauliflower row. He wondered whether he should start planting the celery. But at that moment his little radio emitted a few notes of the national anthem and a woman began to read the 5:00 P.M. news. Paul welcomed the sound of her voice, for it meant that the day's work was done.

He picked up his hoe and walked quickly toward the shed. As he went, he looked at the black furrows with satisfaction. Yesterday he had enriched the soil with sheep manure, nicely rotted, and he knew that the big Snowball cauliflowers would come up with fine white buds, firm and flavoursome.

In the shed he removed his rubber boots, put on his torn canvas shoes, and headed for the elevators. The damn things hadn't been working at lunchtime, but maybe they would be repaired by now. If not, he would again have to walk down eighteen flights of stairs. There were certain advantages to working in this very prestigious indoor farm, but sometimes the vagaries of the elevators made him wonder whether he shouldn't look for a completely different kind of job.

At the landing the sign was still there – *HORS DE SERVICE*. A glum group of workers trooped down the wide staircase. Paul fell in with Chucky Dwyer, who worked in carrots and parsnips, on the floor above. Chucky was twenty-four – two years older than Paul.

"When do you suppose they'll have the elevators fixed?" Paul asked.

"They don't need fixing," Chucky said. "There's nothing wrong with them."

"What do you mean?"

"They've been turned off. To save electricity."

Paul found this hard to believe. After all, this was no shoestring operation, this was the mighty Sun Life Building, in the heart of downtown Montreal. This was the structure that once boasted of being the largest office building in the British Commonwealth. Now, transformed into a farm, it had become a showplace for the Quebec government. Surely they wouldn't be stupid enough to cripple the elevators on purpose.

It was only two years since a special presidential ordinance had decreed that the building be converted to agriculture, and the government was immensely proud of the quality of the loam it had deposited on the marble floors, of the ceiling-based irrigation system it had installed, and of the powerful lights it had brought in to provide synthetic sunshine, day and night. It was a major enterprise – twenty-six storeys, each with more than an acre of first-class farm-floor.

"Want a parsnip?" said Chucky Dwyer, producing one from his overalls, as they trudged down past the fourteenth floor.

"Jesus, Chucky, take it easy," said Paul. There were severe penalties for the pilfering of produce.

11

"Down with the French!" Chucky said, in a low voice, as he bit into the tangy young parsnip.

As they passed the twelfth floor, Paul tried to visualize, as he often did, the things that must have gone on here in the old days, before the separation of Quebec. Mighty capitalists must have walked these floors, issuing orders to seductive secretaries, for this building had housed some of the greatest corporations in Canada, corporations that dealt in oil and titanium, timber and gold. And, of course, insurance: from this building, policies were sold in thirty-four different countries.

Some of this activity continued after Separation, but eventually it started to wither away, unable to survive the increasingly baroque regulations that kept being imposed on business by the bureaucrats of the young republic. One by one the building's typewriters fell silent; one by one the computers were switched off and carted away, to be sold at auction to buyers from Nicaragua and Honduras. Finally, eight years ago, the last of the telex machines was unplugged from the circuits that went round the world.

The massive building stood empty for six years. Then the Minister of Agriculture had his splendid idea. It was truly a seminal idea, whose time had come, for Quebec's lack of foreign exchange and its embittered relations with the United States meant that out-of-season fruit and vegetables could no longer be imported from California. But here was a way to grow them at home, despite the harshness of Quebec's winters.

So far every aspect of *l'agriculture urbaine* was deemed a success, except for the fact that it was proving to be extremely costly to operate. Thus out-of-season produce grown in the Sun Life Building was so expensive that only government officials and army officers could afford to eat it. But the Minister of Agriculture felt that if the scheme could be expanded costs would come down. And expansion was eminently feasible, for with each passing month more office buildings became available for agriculture. There was even talk of the former Bank of

12

Commerce tower – all forty-five storeys of it – being turned over to the raising of chickens.

Wearily, Paul Pritchard and Chucky Dwyer continued down the staircase. When they reached the eighth floor, Chucky caught hold of Paul's elbow. "Let's go in here for a minute," he said, in a conspiratorial tone.

They entered a brightly-lit floor that was devoted entirely to the growing of tomatoes. They were very large tomatoes – Beefsteaks, Marglobes, Big Boy Hybrids – and they were ready for picking. There was no one else in sight.

"Sexy, eh?" said Chucky, examining a Marglobe.

"Magnificent," said Paul.

"Let's take some home, shall we?" said Chucky, darting over to the Big Boy Hybrids.

"You're out of your mind," said Paul. "You'll never get away with it." Two giant tomatoes, of the sort Chucky had just snatched off the vine, could never be smuggled out of the building. The Agricultural Police at the front door were always on the alert, and the slightest bulge in one's overalls led to a close body-search.

"Come over here and cover me," said Chucky, bounding over to a window and putting the tomatoes down on the ledge. He showed Paul where to stand to shield him from the view of anyone who might look in from the staircase. Then Chucky reached into his overalls and took out a sheet of waxed paper and a sharp pocket knife. He quickly cut the tomatoes into neat slices and laid them out on the waxed paper. He took out a second sheet of waxed paper and put it on top of the slices. Then he produced a roll of adhesive tape and handed it to Paul. He unhitched his overalls, opened his shirt, and exposed his chest.

"Tape it to me," said Chucky.

Working quickly, Paul taped the waxed-paper envelope, with its precious contents, to Chucky's chest. Fortunately the chest was not too hairy. Then Chucky buttoned his shirt, hitched up his overalls, and hunched his shoulders a few times.

"It's very comfortable," said Chucky. "I stayed up half the night figuring it out."

"Incredible," said Paul.

"Now a couple for you," said Chucky, darting back to the tomato plants. And, as Chucky started slicing another enormous Big Boy, Paul unhitched his overalls and opened his shirt. A few minutes later they were sauntering out the front door, exchanging pleasantries with the two officers of the Agricultural Police who were stationed there. Then they walked down the broad granite steps and into the street.

"I hear we're getting twenty-one paid holidays next month," said Chucky. "In honour of the glorious anniversary of our getting fucked."

"Not twenty-one," said Paul. "Only nine."

"I read twenty-one in the paper."

"That's been changed. I just heard it on the radio. The French get twenty-one, the Anglos get nine."

"You're kidding!"

"Honest to God. They say it's out of consideration for the feelings of the Anglos. They don't think we'd like to join in on what they call their big Theme Days, where the theme is the Defeat of Anglo Imperialism, the End of Anglo Exploitation of the Workers, etcetera, etcetera."

"The rotten sons of bitches!"

"They say we'd be happier working, on those Theme Days."

"Anything to screw the Anglos, eh? What bastards!"

In Montreal, the term "Anglo-Saxon" had shrunk to "Anglo" and this word had taken on a very broad meaning. If you were of English descent you were, of course, an Anglo. But you were also an Anglo if you were of Irish descent. And you were an Anglo if you were a Jew. Or a Greek or a Serb or an Italian. In fact the term Anglo now applied to anyone at all who had the misfortune not to be French.

Paul and Chucky reached the southwest corner of the Sun Life Building, where they tethered their bicycles every day.

14

The bicycle rack stood under the building's big cornerstone, which bore a deeply-chiselled message: THIS STONE WAS LAID ON MAY 13TH, 1914, BY ROBERTSON MACAULAY, EXECUTIVE HEAD OF THE COMPANY SINCE 1874. This inscription had miraculously escaped the attention of the *Bureau pour la rectification des monuments historiques*, which was devoted to obliterating statements of this sort, all over town, and replacing them with plaques recalling the oppression of the French, before Separation.

"Where are you now, Robbie Macaulay, now that we need you?" said Chucky Dwyer. It was traditional, as you unchained your bicycle, to address this long-departed cornerstone-layer.

"I wonder what he was really like," said Paul.

"He didn't take any shit, I can tell you that," said Chucky.

"No, I guess not."

"He'd just as soon kick them in the ass as look at them. Am I right, Robertson, old boy?"

Paul and Chucky got on their bicycles and started off down the hill. As they went, Paul breathed deeply of the warm spring air. It was marvellously fresh and it smelled of the season's new grass. It reminded him of how his father was always praising the fresh air of Montreal.

"This air is like a tonic," Edward Pritchard would say. "When they wrecked the economy the one thing that got better was the air. No factories, no cars — it's wonderful. The return of the horse — a little aroma of manure in the air — it *humanizes* a city. You young people wouldn't remember what it was like when we had thousands and thousands of cars and trucks and buses, all running on that filthy gasoline. If you took a deep breath downtown it was enough to choke you."

Now, of course, the buses were electrobuses, smooth and non-polluting, running on Quebec's sole source of energy, hydro power from James Bay. The cars were electrocars, but there were very few of them; only high government officials and diplomats could afford them.

Visitors to Montreal were enchanted by the cleanness of the

air. And they always commented on something else that was too familiar to be noticed by Montrealers – the fact that the city *sounded* different from other cities. The continuous, surly growl of the internal combustion engine had disappeared, to be replaced by the gentle tinkle of bicycle bells and the clip-clop of horses' hooves. Added to this, but not too often, was the curious little *wheep-wheep* of an electrocar, sounding its whistle as it glided like a phantom through the quiet, post-industrial streets.

As they pedalled homeward, through these streets, Paul Pritchard became aware of something going wrong with the tomato slices that were taped to his chest. Yes, a thin trickle of tomato juice was working its way down over his stomach and into his crotch. He reached into his shirt and adjusted the strips of adhesive tape. The trickle stopped.

"I've really got to thank you for getting me these tomatoes," Paul said to Chucky.

"Don't thank me," said Chucky. "Thank your government, from whom all blessings flow."

These precious tomatoes, Paul thought, were a good omen. The Spaniards used to call them love apples, didn't they? Well, tonight he would share them with Mona, and she would be thrilled to sample such a rare food. And after they ate, perhaps they would go to bed and make love – for the first time. He had been thinking about that all day.

When they reached Rue Notre-Dame, Chucky veered off to the right. "See you tomorrow," he said, and he pedalled away.

As Paul proceeded on his own route, he could think only of Mona. Last night, sitting on their usual park bench, in the darkest part of the park, their kisses and caresses had become more impassioned than they had ever been before.

"We love each other," Paul had said. "We should go to bed together."

"Yes," Mona had said. "I think we should."

"When?"

"Well, it won't be easy, will it?"

16

"No, I guess not."

It wouldn't be easy because they had nowhere to go. Each had a roommate and each roommate spent a lot of time at home.

"I'll try to get rid of Sorenson," Paul had said. "Tomorrow night."

"Yes, or I'll get rid of Cathy."

Now, as he pedalled homeward, Paul's heart pounded as he thought of those words: "I'll get rid of Cathy." It was a flat, matter-of-fact statement, but it was also pure poetry, evoking visions of flesh against flesh, rapture beyond description.

But what if Mona had changed her mind? It was a terrible thought, and it tormented him for a while, but then he took courage from the memory of how aroused she had been last night, how moist and glistening her lips had been in the moonlight, and how deep her breathing as he slid his hand under her sweater to find her lovely, naked breasts.

As he thought of these things, pedalling all the while, he became aware again of his crotch. There must have been a fair amount of tomato juice down there by this time, and it was becoming quite sticky. He would have to take a bath as soon as he got home. He pedalled hard, racing to get there before the evening line-up formed outside the bathroom, in the boarding house where both he and Mona lived.

Standing on the pedals, swinging vigorously from side to side, Paul went up the long incline that led out of the tunnel and onto Rue Camille Laurin, which the Anglos stubbornly persisted in calling by its original name, Wellington Street. This was the main artery leading to neighbourhoods that once bore names like Point St. Charles, Verdun, Crawford Park, Lasalle. Now it was all lumped together and called the Région Sud-Ouest.

It was a melancholy area of grimy streets and sordid back alleys. Many of the decrepit brick houses were a century old, with sagging floors and collapsing balconies. Here, in the summer, through the hot and crowded streets, the evening breeze carried a sour whiff of garbage with it. And it was here, and in equally desolate areas farther out along the shores of Lake St. Louis, that most of Montreal's Anglos now lived, in varying degrees of poverty—the same Anglos who had once been the lords and masters of Quebec.

2

Mona Rosenstein looked up from her sewing machine at the clock above the door. It was still more than an hour until quitting time and all the other girls in the room were sewing furiously. Their output for the day would be large and praiseworthy, but Mona's would be small. She had been daydreaming all afternoon and thinking about Paul Pritchard. Would they go to bed together tonight? Was it a good idea? She hadn't decided yet.

"*Chris, Mona, n'as tu pas fini tes mo-ziss de manchettes?*" It was Madame Tousignant, the supervisor, anxious for Mona to finish the dress she was working on.

"*Ça sera pas long, Madame Tousignant,*" said Mona. "*J'ai encore eu de la misère avec cette Chris de machine.*"

But she couldn't keep blaming it on her sewing machine, which was actually in perfect repair. She must stop daydreaming. With a little grimace at Madame Tousignant, she got back to work on the elaborately ruffled cuffs she was making.

Mona was one of only two Anglos who were privileged to work as seamstresses at *l'Atelier national du costume*, the state-run workshop that made costumes for the National Theatre, the National Opera, television, and the film industry, such as it was. Thanks to preposterous deadlines, the work here was always nerve-wracking, but during the past few weeks the atmosphere in the big sewing-room had been one of sustained pandemonium. There had never been a work load this big, with more than two thousand costumes needed for the pageants that were being staged for Quebec's twentieth anniversary celebrations.

Now, as she looked around her, Mona saw designers rushing around with their muslins, seamstresses dashing to the storeroom for more cloth, actors trying on doublets and jerkins, and Madame Tousignant making a constant nuisance of herself as she darted about frantically, breathing down everyone's neck.

But Mona was able to ignore the turmoil as she finally concentrated on her work, quickly equalizing the gathers in the ruffled cuffs she had made and sewing each cuff to a leg-of-mutton sleeve. The dress was now finished and she held it up to inspect it. It looked quite good and the actress who wore it would probably be quite convincing as a woman of New France, in the eighteenth century.

"*C'est vraiment beau,*" said Madame Tousignant, snatching the dress from Mona's hands and striding across the room with it. The dress would be used in the Proclamation of Sovereignty pageant, which would be a complex amalgam of historical and allegorical motifs.

Sitting down at her sewing machine again, Mona wondered what garment would be assigned to her next. She looked at the sheet of paper listing the items that would be required for the Proclamation of Sovereignty: blue worsted business suits for the Founding Fathers, overalls for the Allegorical Farmers, oilskins for the Allegorical Fishermen, work-shirts for the Allegorical Workers, blue-jeans for the Patriotic Students, smocks and berets for the Patriotic Artists, robes for the Patriotic Judges, a blindfold for the Statue of Justice, and moneybags (large) for the Allegorical Anglo Capitalists of the Colonial Era.

Looking up from the list, Mona saw that the other seamstresses were getting up from their machines and heading for the door. And she remembered that a special staff meeting had been called. Reluctantly she joined the others as they filed out of the sewing-room and went up a flight of stairs to the auditorium. There they took seats amid a crowd of chattering designers, cutters, and administrators. The noise subsided as the director of *l'Atelier* came out onto the stage, went to the lectern, and began his address.

"*Mesdames, mesdemoiselles, messieurs,*" he said. "By the end of this week we will have finished all the costumes needed for the Proclamation of Sovereignty. I congratulate you on your zeal and devotion, but next week we must take up the biggest challenge of all – the Battle of Pointe Fortune.

"As you all know, this was one of the greatest events in the history of our republic, the day when our glorious flag was first stained by patriotic blood. It will be an inspiring pageant. But the costumes must also be inspiring. And to make them inspiring we must remember that a costume does not merely clothe an actor with authenticity, it also makes a statement, a political statement."

In the audience, Mona was tempted to feign a sarcastic yawn. They had been through this nonsense so often before. She tuned out of the lecture and let her mind drift back to Paul Pritchard, and what might happen between them that night.

At the age of nineteen, Mona had slept with only one man before. She had been thoroughly in love with him and had suffered greatly when, after five months of intimacy, he had left her for another woman. His name was Hugh and for a year she had thought of nothing but Hugh. Would Paul Pritchard be capable of making her as miserable as Hugh had? No, she thought not. Did that mean, then, that she was not really in love with Paul? Or did it mean she was older now, tougher, more resilient? Yes, that was it – tougher and more resilient.

"Our designers," the director was saying, "have completed their preliminary sketches for the Battle of Pointe Fortune. May we have the first slide, please?" The lights in the auditorium dimmed and on the screen there appeared a drawing of a man in a ridiculous, tent-like red coat.

"This Royal Canadian Mounted Policeman," said the director, "typifies the cowardice of the enemy. You will notice that the red tunic, which was generally tight-fitting and ended just below the hips, has been considerably loosened and now

21

reaches to the knee. A coward needs loose, baggy clothes to make it easier for him to run away. You will also note the policeman's hat. Historical purists may say that this hat had a wide, stiff brim, but they are correct only in an unimaginative, literal way. A higher truth – allegorical truth – tells us that it cannot have been a stiff brim because stiffness suggests firmness and resolve. Thus, in our pageant, the frightened RCMP officer wears a hat with a loose, floppy brim – a brim that speaks of a certain sexual ambiguity. Next slide, please."

The next few slides showed sketches of Canadian soldiers in a variety of uniforms, all of them made preposterous in one way or another. Then came grotesque sketches of the merchants of Pointe Fortune, who were said to have made a great deal of money selling beer, at hugely inflated prices, to the fighting men of both sides.

"And now for the gallant defenders of the Republic of Quebec," the director was saying. "Next slide, please."

The next sketches were of members of the old Quebec provincial police, wearing uniforms that reminded Mona of the creations of the great Paris couturiers of the 1970s. The officers might have been dressed by Yves St. Laurent in one of his flamboyant periods, while the uniforms of the other ranks seemed derived from the more simple lines of Givenchy or Courrèges.

"These are the uniforms of men who were prepared to lay down their lives for Quebec," the director was saying. "Now let us briefly review the course of the great battle itself, so that the noble memory of it will inspire you as you work."

The director then launched into a lengthy account of the Battle of Pointe Fortune, the young republic's only military engagement to date. And Mona listened with mounting annoyance as he repeated the familiar official version of the story, which was almost entirely fiction. But soon her mind drifted back to Paul again, to thoughts of how strong he was, how solid and dependable.

Paul was the kind of man who would make a good husband.

Somehow the idea made her uncomfortable. She didn't want to get married, did she? But why not? What if Paul asked her to? She turned these questions around in her mind, handling them gingerly. And then she remembered the excitement Paul was able to create in her body. Surely they could sleep together before she had all the answers to all the questions.

"And that, dear colleagues," the director was saying, "was how it happened in that great battle of twenty years ago. Let your hands remember its glory each time you snip your scissors; let your fingers remember its beauty each time you baste a hem."

And let your lies choke you, thought Mona, and may your lips turn green. She pointedly refrained from joining in the applause that her co-workers were bestowing on the director. She got to her feet, anxious to leave the auditorium, but just then she heard her name on the public address system: "*Est-ce que Mademoiselle Rosenstein aura la bonté de me voir dans mon bureau?*"

The bastard was asking her to come to his office. Could it be that he had noticed her not applauding and that he considered this an act of political defiance? That was not impossible. But it was more likely that his vanity was involved, not his ideology. Before he became director of *l'Atelier*, Rodrigue Martineau had been a very unsuccessful actor, and it was widely believed that he called these frequent assemblies in the auditorium mainly to assuage his recurring hunger for a bit of applause.

"*Ah, la belle Mona,*" said Martineau, as his secretary showed her into his enormous office. "*Assieds-toi.*" He gestured at the chair at the other side of his desk.

Martineau looked very much a man of the theatre, with handsome features that Mona found too perfect to be interesting. Although he was only in his mid-forties, his hair had gone completely silver-grey; it was a massive crown of hair, painstakingly sculptured three times a week by his hairdresser. His clothes looked as though they had been made in Europe, rather than in Quebec, perhaps because the best designer at *l'Atelier* spent all his time illicitly making suits and shirts for Martineau and dresses for Martineau's wife, mistress, and girlfriends.

"And how is the elegant Mona today?" he said, his hand darting to his temple to check his coiffure.

"I'm fine, thank you," said Mona, quickly deciding not to ask him how *he* was.

"I have been looking through your sketches," he said. "They are extremely interesting."

"Oh? . . . thank you," said Mona. She was surprised. She had given him the sketches only that morning.

"So you want to be a designer," he said. "The creativity of the artist's pencil as opposed to the drudgery of the needle and thread. Is that it?"

"Yes," she said. "I think I would be of more use to you as a designer."

"But you haven't got your certificate. Am I correct?"

"That's right. I failed the exam."

"And you would like me to get you a certificate. Through the back door, as it were. Is that right?"

"Yes," said Mona.

"Well, that is not impossible." He picked up the sheaf of drawings Mona had given him and flipped through them. Mona watched him carefully. This was a tremendous development. He had just admitted that he could get her, illegally, a Certificate of Linguistic Purity. This would allow her to rise to Grade 3 in the civil service and, in theory, she could then become a designer. Otherwise she would be stuck at Grade 2 for the rest of her life, a robot at a sewing machine.

"Your drawings show imagination and flair," said Martineau. "Some of them, however, lack historical accuracy."

"Oh? Which ones?"

"This one, for instance: 'Heroine of the Textile Factory Strike in the Colonial Era.'" He pushed the drawing across the desk toward Mona. It showed one of the allegorical figures participating in the pageants. Mona had done a series of these to prove how much better she was than some of the designers who

24

were long established on the staff of *l'Atelier*.

"This heroine is not quite right," said Martineau.

"What's wrong with her?"

"The textile strikers were extremely feminine. Yours is not."

"In what way?"

"You have made her breasts too small."

"I don't agree. They're perfectly normal."

"A heroine in a textile strike should have large, firm breasts – magnificent breasts. Not little cupcakes like these. Nature has been very generous to *you*, my dear Mona, so why have you been so stingy with our heroine? Is it because she is French?"

"No, of course not."

"Also, I get the impression that the textile heroine, as you have drawn her, is wearing a brassiere."

Martineau had been staring at Mona's bosom all the time he was talking. She pretended not to notice and sat stock still, biting her lip and resisting an impulse to get up and storm out of the office.

"But she would never have worn a brassiere," Martineau was saying. "In those days they were considered to be symbolic of the exploitation of women."

"What makes you think she's wearing one?" said Mona. She might as well go along with this a bit further; it might mean getting that precious certificate.

"If she were free of the constrictions of a brassiere," said Martineau, "she would present a...a more pointed appearance. There would be fascinating little ripples in the fabric of her dress."

Martineau was still gazing shamelessly at Mona's chest and she remembered that the blouse she was wearing was rather tight. She herself never wore a bra and obviously Martineau was seeing something in the thin nylon of her blouse that was exciting him. She thought for a moment of crossing her arms in front of her bosom, to hide it from him, but then she decided

25

not to. To hell with him. She sat straight in her chair, aware that her anger was making her breathe deeply, causing her breasts to heave and stand out even more.

"*Magnifique*," said Martineau, dreamily. And, with the sort of gesture that had contributed to his failure as an actor, he licked his upper lip with the tip of his tongue.

"Will you get me the certificate?" said Mona.

"Perhaps," he said. He stared into her eyes for a moment but when he spoke he was crisp and businesslike. "I would have to be convinced that you are not a complete egotist about your work. You would have to be willing to be part of a team. At *l'Atelier* everything is teamwork, is it not?"

"I *can* work on a team. In fact I like it that way."

"You would have to work with *me*. On these sketches, for instance. I want them modified in certain ways. I have already mentioned the textile heroine. There are other changes as well. Could we do that?"

"Yes, why not?"

"What I suggest," said Martineau, "is that we get away from this hectic environment and go somewhere quiet, where we can work. I have a lovely little ski cabin in the Laurentians. We could leave on Saturday morning and come back Sunday night. In the beautiful quiet of the mountains, the moth will become a butterfly, the seamstress will become a designer. Is that not a splendid idea?"

"No," said Mona, getting to her feet, "it is not a splendid idea."

Martineau sighed, theatrically. "You Anglos make life so difficult for yourselves," he said. "But there is no need for you to make your decision right away. Think it over. The offer remains open." He smiled broadly and handed Mona her sketches. As she took them she noticed the silky, cream-coloured double cuffs of his shirt. Almost everyone in Quebec, the French as well as the Anglos, wore clothes made from the cheapest synthetic fabrics, imported from North Korea or Albania. But Martineau wore only cotton or silk or wool, all of it no

26

doubt smuggled in from the United States. And his creamy cuffs were ostentatiously stitched with chocolate-coloured thread.

"Think it over," he said, as he held the office door open for her. "You could have a very exciting future as a designer."

As she went down the stairs toward the sewing-room, Mona felt her hands shaking with anger. The sketch of the textile heroine fell from her sheaf of drawings and, after a moment's hesitation, she left it on the stairs and continued down. By the time she got to the sewing-room she had no drawings at all left in her hand; instead they lay behind her, in a trail along the floor and up the stairs. They represented weeks of work, late at night.

In the sewing-room she found that all the other seamstresses had gone home. She sat down at her machine, an isolated and vulnerable figure in the middle of the big room. Outside, the sun was setting and the gloom of evening was starting to creep in through the windows. As she sat, her head in her hands, her anger started to give way to despair. This had almost certainly been her last chance to get the Certificate of Linguistic Purity. She had already failed the examination twice and the only way to succeed, obviously, was to sleep with Martineau or someone like him. But she would never do that. And so, like almost every other Anglo, she was doomed to work for the rest of her life at a job that paid the lowest of wages – cheap Anglo labour for the French overlords.

3

When she came out of *l'Atelier*, Mona found that her bicycle was the only one left in the rack. She unchained it and pedalled away, down Avenue des Pins. Soon she would be with Paul and she was anxious to talk to him, once again, about the doubts she had regarding her job.

Should she quit? On days like this *l'Atelier* filled her with revulsion. Martineau was right when he said that every snip of the scissors, every stitch of the needle furthered the cause of Quebec nationalism. Surely, then, she was a traitor to her own people, who were being so impoverished and so humiliated by this same loathsome nationalism. It was a thought that frequently tormented her.

But if she left *l'Atelier*, what could she do? Become just another Anglo maid in one of the big French houses in Westmount? Become a drudge in a sweltering laundry, or in a grimy shoe factory? Or should she follow in the footsteps of her sister Naomi, who was bitterly critical of her for working at *l'Atelier*? Naomi, noble and uncompromising, spent her days sorting old rags and bottles, and washing the bottles so they could be re-used.

No, thought Mona, I will not wash out the beer bottles of the French. I will become a brilliant designer of costumes, a woman of the theatre, and in that way I will help my people rediscover their heritage and their pride.

She was thinking of the rumours that the authorities might soon permit a limited revival of English theatre in Montreal – "the folklore of the minority culture," as they called it. If that came to pass, Mona would surely have an important contri-

28

bution to make. She would beg and borrow ration coupons wherever she could, and with them she would buy cloth and make magnificent costumes for *The Tempest* and *Hamlet*. A whole generation of young Anglos would become aware of the existence of Shakespeare and Shaw and O'Neill. It might stir them out of their slavish feelings of inferiority.

But, as she pedalled on in the dusk, Mona wondered whether she was not paying too big a price to learn her trade. Next week she would be sewing costumes for the re-enactment of the Battle of Pointe Fortune; she would be helping to reiterate a maddening falsehood that was presented as gospel by all Quebec textbooks. How could she justify this?

The Battle of Pointe Fortune . . . she wondered how many Anglos knew the truth of what had really happened there, on the border between Quebec and Ontario, twenty years ago. Mona knew, and knew with certainty, for her father had told her about it. Her father and her mother had actually been at Pointe Fortune on that infamous June twenty-sixth, in the year before Mona was born.

Jack and Gloria Rosenstein had been married in May. The Separatist victory in the Referendum of June 24 came as an alarming surprise to them, as it did to all the Anglos of Montreal. The abrupt Proclamation of Sovereignty the next day came as another shock. But the most painful surprise of all was the immediate reaction of the Government of Canada; the Rosensteins watched in consternation as the Prime Minister came on television and announced that the borders between Quebec and the rest of Canada had been closed. There would be no trade with Quebec and no immigration from Quebec. Canada was already beset by record unemployment and the arrival of hundreds of thousands of Anglo refugees would be disastrous.

"But there is a more important reason," said the Prime Minister. "You Anglos must stay in Quebec – and fight. You must help bring Quebec back to its senses, back into the Confederation that – "

"The son of a bitch!" said Jack Rosenstein.

29

That night the Rosensteins locked up their apartment, got into their Dodge Aspen, and drove out onto the Trans-Canada Highway in the direction of the Ontario border. They turned off the highway at Rigaud and felt their way cautiously along Route 342. Just outside the village of Pointe Fortune they abandoned the car, climbed a farmer's fence and started across the fields. On their backs were knapsacks containing a change of clothes and a few prized possessions. In their pockets they had nineteen hundred dollars, their total savings.

It was a clear night, with a crescent moon and a sky full of stars. Jack felt that if they kept the North Star on their right, always at the same angle, they would be going westward. By dawn they would be many miles into Ontario. Somehow they would find their way to Ottawa and there they could "fade into the woodwork," as Jack put it. They would find jobs in Ottawa, or in Toronto, or maybe in the States.

The hike across the fields was not an easy one. They kept stumbling into holes and cutting themselves with brambles. There seemed to be innumerable barbed-wire fences to get through. After two hours they were exhausted. They sank to the ground to rest and to eat their chocolate bars.

"Maybe we're making a mistake," said Gloria. "Maybe we should've stayed."

"We're not making a mistake," said Jack.

"I know, I know. It'll be bad for the Jews."

"There's no doubt about that, kiddo. They're going to have to have *somebody* to blame for the mess they're going to make. So let us not make ourselves available for that honour. When the economy comes to a halt, let them blame the Eskimos."

They got to their feet and started walking again, but a few minutes later they heard the barking of dogs, and a searchlight came on. Its bright beam moved slowly across the field until it found them. "Please stay where you are," came a voice on a bullhorn. "Do not move. Do not attempt to run." It was the RCMP.

30

The Mounties put them into a Land Rover and they bounced across the field and down a dirt road. They reached a large barn, which was brightly lit, and they got out. Inside the barn there were almost two hundred other captured Anglo refugees, including many small children. Among them was Lloyd Cameron, who worked for the same company that Jack did.

"What's going on, Lloyd?" Jack asked.

"We're screwed, that's all," said Cameron.

"If we can't get into Ontario why don't we go to the States?"

"We can't do that either," said Cameron. "It just came over the radio that the Americans have closed their border too – at the request of the Canadian government."

"Then we *are* screwed."

"We're supposed to go home and fight."

"Screwed, blewed, and tattooed."

Soon after dawn, three buses pulled up at the barn and the refugees were herded aboard. Twenty minutes later they were approaching the Quebec border. But on the outskirts of Pointe Fortune they came to a stop. Five patrol cars of the Quebec Police Force were parked in a row across the road, completely blocking it. A QPF captain, swagger-stick under his arm, was standing in the middle of the road, facing the convoy coming from Ontario. The convoy came to a halt and an RCMP officer got out and walked across to the QPF captain.

"Listen, Philippe," the Mountie said, looking slightly embarrassed, "would you please move your cars?"

"*Qui êtes-vous et qu'est-ce que vous voulez?*" said the QPF man.

"Oh, for Chrissakes, Philippe," said the Mountie, "you know damn well who I am."

"*Je regrette mais la frontière de la République est fermée,*" said the Quebec policeman. And he read aloud from a Telex he had just received from Quebec City. It said that the Republic of Quebec would do everything it could to help Anglos exercise their God-given right to leave the Republic. And it would do

31

everything possible to prevent their forcible repatriation by the Canadian authorities.

The Mountie and the Quebec policeman argued for a few minutes and then the Mountie went back to his car, where he spoke briefly into the radio. Twenty minutes later the Canadian Armed Forces arrived, rumbling down the road in armoured personnel carriers. With them were two Leopard tanks, which headed straight for the Quebec police cars that were blocking the road. Metal crumpled and glass splintered as the tanks crashed into the cars and pushed them out of the way. Then the RCMP buses, with the refugees aboard, drove down the main street of Pointe Fortune into Quebec.

It was at this moment that a shot rang out and a bullet bounced off one of the tanks. There was silence for a second or two and then came a brief burst of machine-gun fire from one of the personnel carriers. And then there was quiet again.

This was the extent of the Battle of Pointe Fortune. The windows of a tavern and an undertaking parlour were shattered and a certain Sergeant Brisebois of the Quebec police was wounded. His was the only blood that flowed that day, from a shallow flesh wound in the left buttock, but in the years to come these meagre events were to provide an inexhaustible source of raw material for Quebec's historians, film makers and balladeers. Sergeant Brisebois was immortalized as a warrior who had been "prepared to give his life" to repel an invasion by fascist forces from Canada. And the *Bureau du symbolisme national* came up with a tattered *fleur-de-lys* flag, one corner of which was stained dark red, allegedly with patriotic gore from the wound of Sergeant Brisebois. The flag was framed in heavy gilt and hung in the Grand Reception Hall of the Presidential Mansion.

At Pointe Fortune that day, after the tanks crashed through, the RCMP buses drove three miles into Quebec, where they discharged the Anglo refugees. Then they turned around and went back to Ontario. Jack and Gloria Rosenstein found the Dodge Aspen they had abandoned the night before and drove

32

back to Montreal. They still had the key to their apartment. And that night, as they sought solace in each other's arms, their daughter Mona was conceived.

In the months and years that followed, the borders of Canada remained tightly closed to the Anglos of Quebec who, to their dismay, found that they were being increasingly despised by their fellow countrymen. After all, said the Canadians, was it not these Anglos who were the actual *cause* of Separation? Was it not the Montreal Anglos, with their insatiable greed, who had exploited the poor French Canadians for two whole centuries? Was it not these arrogant Anglos who had persistently refused to sample the vibrant culture of the French majority? "Canadians from sea to sea," said the Toronto *Globe and Mail*, "always felt a great warmth for their Québécois brothers and sisters. The only coldness was in the heart of the Montreal Anglo."

This theme was taken up by the journalists of many countries who came to write about Quebec soon after Separation. Readers in Hamburg, Buenos Aires, and New Delhi learned how, in the Colonial Era, the French had been denied the sidewalks of Montreal and had had to walk in the gutters; how the eating of pea soup had been forbidden; how, in the great Anglo manor houses of Verdun and Ville Emard, haughty young scions would impregnate terrified French parlourmaids and then cast them aside like worn-out riding boots. The London *Observer* spoke of a "dark, perverse stain" in the character of the Montreal Anglos who, like the Afrikaners of South Africa, had been cut off for too many centuries from the humanist culture of their mother country.

Almost everywhere in the world there was admiration for the courage of the young Quebec republic and contempt for the Anglos, who were reaping a reward that was held to be richly deserved. In Montreal, the English newspapers reprinted the most lurid of the foreign attacks on their people, without comment. For even the Montreal Anglos themselves were starting to believe it.

33

One evening, Jack Rosenstein put down his newspaper with tears in his eyes. "You know what we are?" he said to his wife. "We are the wretched of the earth."

And in her crib, the baby Mona wailed and wept, prophetically.

* * *

In the years after Separation, Canada gradually lost the will to exist as a nation. Nova Scotia and New Brunswick were the first provinces to seek admission to the American union, although they had little hope of being accepted. The Americans had been paying more attention than ever before to their neighbours to the north and American commentators seemed finally to have discerned the elusive qualities of Canada's national character – cantankerousness, masochism, and an insatiable need to complain. For many Americans the situation was summed up by a much-quoted editorial in the New York *Daily News* that carried the headline "Who Needs Them?"

But in Washington, the administration pointed out that the United States *did* need Canada – or what was left of it – very badly indeed. For Canada possessed, in its huge lakes and rivers, almost half of all the world's fresh water. And the United States was running out of water – a commodity that was required in enormous quantities to cool nuclear reactors.

Nova Scotia and New Brunswick were thus grudgingly accepted into the Union. And, as each year passed, another province or two gave up the ghost and joined the United States. On the day that Alberta became the fifty-sixth state, the *Toronto Star* printed the cartoon with the immortal caption – "Will the Last One Out Please Turn Off the Lights?"

On the day the lights were finally turned off – by Ontario – Jack Rosenstein put down his newspaper and stared out the window for a long time. "As of today," he said to his wife, "the Anglos are completely alone in this world."

Alone, but not forgotten. In the United States, whenever there was a move to increase the tiny annual quota of Montreal

Anglos to be admitted as immigrants, there was fierce opposition by congressmen from the Canadian States, who used words like "racist" and "moral turpitude" in their filibusters. In the end, the Canadian congressmen always had their way.

The rich Montreal Anglos – about one per cent of the Anglo population – had sent their money out of Quebec long before the Final Referendum. And when Separation finally came, these people were able to settle very comfortably in Bermuda or Nassau or the south of France. But for Anglos who were poor, and for the middle class, there were few avenues of escape. This group had no choice but to remain in the new republic, a captive minority doomed to stew in its own juice.

*   *   *

As she emerged from the tunnel and pedalled down Wellington Street, Mona Rosenstein found herself thinking of escape from Quebec. She had often thought of it in the past, but now the idea had a new dimension: perhaps Paul Pritchard would come with her. Together they would make a new life for themselves – in New York or maybe California. Together they would become snowbacks.

It was only in the dead of winter, during the fiercest blizzards, that Anglos had much hope of getting across the tightly-guarded border and into Vermont. In the summer, or even in good winter weather, the United States Border Patrol was diabolically efficient; but during a raging snowstorm its helicopters were grounded and its electronic sensing devices were much less effective than usual. If the weather was bad enough, snowbacks from Quebec were said to have a fifty-fifty chance.

Mona visualized herself with Paul, eight or nine months from now, when it would be winter again. It would be midnight and they would be sitting in the kitchen of a lonely farmhouse a mile or two from the border. As they warmed themselves at the pot-bellied stove, storing warmth for the ordeal ahead, the well-bribed old farmer would be looking out the window, his practised eye watching for signs that the storm was reaching its peak. Finally he would say, "*Maintenant*," and he would hold the door open for them. "*Bonne chance*," he would say, as they went into the night.

The wind would be howling and the snow would be swirling, a maelstrom of icy particles to lash their faces and blind their eyes. Quickly they would fasten the thongs of their snowshoes around their moccasins. Over their warm clothes they would be wearing hooded robes made of bedsheets, ghostly garments that would make them blend into the turbulent snowscape – white on white, invisible, inaudible.

As they plunged on southwards, toward the Green Mountains of Vermont, Mona would draw strength from a vision she would see in the midst of the blizzard, a vision involving the bright lights of Broadway and the excitement of a theatre lobby, during intermission, on opening night. "This is Mona Rosenstein, the designer," somebody would be saying. "Congratulations!" the dapper old gentleman would say. "If the play was half as good as the costumes, they'd have a hit on their hands. You wouldn't by any chance be interested in designing for motion pictures, would you?"

The bright lights of Broadway – they were only six hundred kilometres from where she was now, bicycling along the shabby and poorly-lit Wellington Street. She pedalled faster; only four more blocks to go and then she'd be home, at the boarding house where she and Paul lived. As soon as they were alone, she would ask him what he thought of this bold and exciting idea: that they say farewell to this dreary homeland of theirs and set out as snowbacks together, in search of a better life.

4

"For God's sake, Pritchard, will you hurry up?" Colin Armitage was shouting and banging on the door.

"I just got in," said Paul, from inside the bathroom.

"A likely story," said Armitage. "Your time is up."

"I'm sorry," said Paul. "I forgot to start the timer."

"Well, I'm starting it now, buddy," said Armitage. "And I'm coming back in four minutes. But the next time this happens I'm going to lodge a formal complaint."

Outside the bathroom, Armitage turned the little hourglass around and the sand inside started running down. It was a strict rule in Mrs. MacVicar's boarding house that nobody was to spend more than four minutes at a time in the bathroom. You turned the hourglass over when you went in and you damn well finished your business before the sand ran out. "It's the only way to be fair to everybody," Mrs. MacVicar would say. "A bathroom always gives trouble if there's no rules and regulations."

Inside the bathroom, Paul quickly stripped off his clothes. Then, with great care, he untaped the waxed-paper envelope from his chest. The tomato slices inside it were looking a bit anaemic, having lost a lot of juice during the bicycle ride home. But they would still be very tasty.

Quickly Paul examined the ancient bathtub, running his fingernail through the dark grey ring of grime around the inside. It was thick and crusty. Four minutes was not nearly enough time to scrub it away, fill the tub and bathe. Once again, a shower would have to do. He turned on the shower and tested the water with his hand. It was ice cold. He had forgotten that this was neither a Wednesday nor a Sunday, so there was no hot water. Grimacing, he went to the sink, moistened his washcloth and started swabbing away at the sticky tomato-juice residue on his stomach.

When he came out of the bathroom, Paul found Armitage waiting impatiently. Armitage was obviously going in for another four-minute read; he had his newspaper in one hand and his roll of toilet paper in the other. Whenever you passed the bathroom, Armitage seemed to be there – either going in or coming out or waiting – but his toilet paper roll never seemed to get any smaller. His constipation was legendary.

As Armitage turned the hourglass and nipped into the bathroom, Paul saw Doreen Brewster coming down the hall in her flashy green dressing gown. He noticed that the toilet paper roll she was carrying was pink, the most expensive kind. Nobody else at Mrs. MacVicar's ever used pink.

"Who's inside?" said Doreen.

"Armitage," said Paul.

"Aw, Christ!" said Doreen. She went to the door and banged on it. "Just don't get too comfortable, Armitage," she said. "I'm out here watching the timer."

Paul went down the hall toward his room. Armitage was now shouting something at Doreen and Paul was glad he couldn't quite make out what was being said. These bathroom altercations always depressed him and they often made him think of looking for another place to live. And yet Mrs. MacVicar's was considered to be one of the best of the many boarding houses that catered to unmarried Anglos. While not exactly clean, it was not as dirty as most and it harboured no vermin more serious than silverfish. The sheets were changed regularly, once every eight weeks, and for a small extra charge you could have a hotplate in your room if you wanted to cook.

The main advantage, however, was that the house was not

overcrowded; the hallways were not teeming with people, as they were in some houses. Paul and Mona each had only one roommate and, although some of the rooms had three people in them, there were no rooms with four or even five inhabitants, as there were across the street at Mrs. McGillivray's. Also, Mrs. McGillivray's had a *three*-minute toilet, which was hardly a drawing card; for a man with Armitage's problem, for example, the extra sixty seconds permitted by Mrs. MacVicar could be crucial.

In his room, Paul carefully laid out the tomato slices on top of his dresser. He glanced at his watch. Mona should be home any minute now. He must quickly do whatever he could to make the room more conducive to romance. His roommate, Bud Sorenson, had assured him in the morning that he wouldn't be home before midnight, so Paul would be able to bring Mona up right after supper. And perhaps, in this room, on that bed, tonight, they would finally make love.

The main problem with the room was the lighting. At the moment this was provided by a single hundred-watt bulb hanging from the centre of the ceiling. The undressing and the actual lovemaking would, of course, take place in the dark, but there would have to be some preliminaries first and it was hard to imagine even the most elementary of these taking place under the glare of this hostile, unfrosted bulb.

Paul thought he had the solution. On the way home he had stopped at a second-hand store and had bought a very cheap table lamp. It was an aged, ramshackle affair but it would do the trick. He put it on the night-table between his bed and Bud Sorenson's, and then he unscrewed the ceiling bulb and put it into the lamp. But the result was disappointing; the lamp had a thin, cream-coloured cardboard shade and the light it gave was still far too harsh. Something would have to be done to darken the shade.

Paul rummaged around in his dresser drawer, hesitated, and then decided to make the sacrifice. Taking a pair of scissors, he cut a wide band of dark blue cloth from the seat of his second-

39

best pair of overalls. Using paper clips, he fastened the cloth around the lampshade. The result was incredibly effective: the lamp now gave off a subtle bluish light, a glow so subdued that you could no longer make out the gaudy pattern in the linoleum on the floor, or the outlines of Bud Sorenson's socks drying above the wash basin. The bedsheets, rather than looking tired and grey, now had a soft, mysterious sheen. Even the air in the room now seemed better, less dominated by the sour aroma of Bud Sorenson's empty beer bottles. In fact, Paul reflected, it was a room that was ready for love.

Except that the door was opening and Bud Sorenson was coming in.

"Is that you, Paul?" he said, peering into the dimly-lit room. "What is this, anyway, Hallowe'en in a whorehouse?"

"Christ, Bud, I thought you were going to be out tonight."

"I was, but I changed my mind."

"Well, that's damn inconvenient for me."

"Sorry, old chap. What the hell happened to our light, any-way?"

In the dimness of the room, Paul saw that Sorenson was lurching around and groping for the light bulb that ought to have been hanging from the ceiling. Sorenson had had a lot to drink.

"I was going to stay uptown," Sorenson said, "but I decided to come home and have a party instead." He produced a large green bottle of De Kuyper's gin from his coat and waved it in the air. Sorenson, a garbage collector by trade, often had a party on payday. A party consisted of him sitting alone in the room, brooding, and drinking a whole bottle of De Kuyper's by himself. As the evening wore on, Sorenson would speak softly to himself, voicing the conversation of dozens of imaginary guests attending the party. They were people from all walks of life — some young, some old, some sophisticated, some coarse; the only thing they all had in common was their ceaseless quest for ever more innovative ways of cursing the French.

"Should be a good party tonight," said Sorenson. "I'm expecting thirty people, including the Chief of Police."

Disgusted, Paul put on his necktie and left the room. He went downstairs to the parlour and was pleased to see Mona sitting on the chesterfield, waiting for him. She had just come in. She looked more beautiful than ever.

"How did it go today?" he said, sitting down beside her.

"Bad news and good news," said Mona. "We've got to talk." Her eyes were bright with excitement, suggesting to Paul that the good news probably outweighed the bad.

But this was obviously not the place to talk, what with four or five other boarders sitting around and watching television as they waited for the supper bell. The antiquated ten-inch black-and-white screen was showing a lengthy news item about President Chartrand sitting for a sculptor who was making a new statue of him, to be unveiled at the twentieth anniversary celebrations.

Colin Armitage came into the parlour and to make room for him on the chesterfield Paul had to move very close to Mona, so that his thigh pressed tightly against hers. The sensation was immensely exciting and when their eyes met he felt sure she was telling him that she was ready to make love that night. If only it wasn't for that accursed Bud Sorenson. He felt a surge of rage when he thought of Sorenson; he would love to run up the stairs, grab him and throw him out the window – and then throw his gin bottle and his dirty socks after him.

"What's the matter?" Mona was whispering. "You look upset."

"It's Sorenson. He promised to go out, but he's staying in."

Mona grimaced and he found some solace in the fact that she too was disappointed. But perhaps *her* roommate could be dislodged.

"What about Cathy?" he whispered. "Is there any chance?"

"No," said Mona. "She's in bed again, refusing to face life."

They looked at each other unhappily. They would not make love tonight. Once again they would go to the park, where they would embrace long and passionately; and then they would

41

come home, frustrated and unfulfilled.

But even if they *could* go to one of their rooms, it wouldn't automatically be clear sailing. Mrs. MacVicar had strict rules about what she called "visitation"; if the visitor was a member of the opposite sex the door was supposed to be kept open at all times, and the visitation was supposed to be over by 10:00 P.M. Like all the other Anglo ladies who kept boarding houses, Mrs. MacVicar was determined that there would be no fornication under her roof. If you were caught doing it, you could be instantly expelled from the house and you acquired a reputation that made it hard to get a room elsewhere. Every year there were three or four expulsions from Mrs. MacVicar's.

In the parlour, somebody had turned off the television and the boarders, as they waited for the supper bell, were once again listening to Mr. Brophy hold forth on the glories of his past life. Mr. Brophy was a milkman, but he had once been an executive in a chemical company. He was in his fifties, a distinguished-looking man in a threadbare suit.

Paul and Mona exchanged a secret yawn as Mr. Brophy reached into his pocket and produced a small plastic rectangle. He handed it to Doreen Brewster, who was relatively new to the house and hadn't heard it all before.

"This is what they used to call a 'credit card' in the old days," he said. "It was your passport to gracious living."

"'Master Charge,'" Doreen said, wonderingly, as she read from the card. She passed it on to Spiro Costakis, who passed it on to Lionel Greenspoon.

"You could get anything with that card," said Mr. Brophy. "You could get clothes and furniture and meals in luxurious restaurants – anything." And he explained to her how it worked.

"I'm not sure I understand," said Doreen. "You say I could walk into a store in London, England, and buy a pair of shoes with this card, without using money. But what if they don't know me in that store? What if I was a total stranger?"

"But the whole point, my dear, is that they *wouldn't* have to know you," said Mr. Brophy. Patiently he explained the whole system once again, in great detail. "And," he said, winding up, "you could collect all those little credit card slips from expensive restaurants and be able to take it off your income tax. You wouldn't know about that, Doreen, but I'm sure Mr. Costakis and Mr. Greenspoon would."

"I suppose you were proud of that," said Greenspoon. "Screwing the government. That's what caused the downfall of Canada."

"Oh, come on, Lionel," said Mr. Brophy. "I wasn't cheating the government. Those were legitimate business expenses. I had to do a lot of entertaining. You forget, Lionel, but I was vice-president of an important company."

"And I was the Queen of Sheba," said Greenspoon.

But it was true. Mr. Brophy had been a vice-president of Richmond, Foster and Clark Limited, a firm that did a world-wide trade in chemicals. He was the youngest vice-president the company had ever had, and it was widely believed that he was destined for the very top.

Richmond, Foster and Clark was one of those Anglo companies that decided to take a chance and stay on in Montreal after Separation. And for nine years they found it surprisingly easy to do business in an independent Quebec. Anglos now referred to that period, nostalgically, as the "Nine Good Years" – a halcyon time before the Great Riots and the humiliations that followed them. During the Nine Good Years it didn't seem to matter to Anglos that they couldn't emigrate to the United States, for life in Quebec was very agreeable.

The key to the good life – and a high salary – was bilingualism. Bilingual executives could do business in Quebec in French, as now required by law, and in English with the rest of the world, where English was the international language of commerce. Mr. Brophy and many other Anglos like him were by now fluently bilingual. They were the children of wise Anglo parents who, as far back as the early 1960s, had responded to the rumblings of Quebec nationalism by making sure that

43

their sons and daughters learned French, and learned it well.

But from the 1960s onwards, while young Anglos in Westmount were busily learning French, the French students in Outremont were becoming defiantly unilingual. Their fathers and grandfathers were all fluent in English, but for this generation it was a badge of honour *not* to be able to speak the language of the colonial oppressors. The French students were obliged to attend English classes in their schools, to be sure, but their teachers – angry, bearded young men – used the English period not to teach the language of Milton but to discuss the writings of Mao Tse-tung, in French.

"It's the most natural thing in the world," Mona's father, Jack Rosenstein, would say. "Only the underdog learns a foreign language, never the overdog. Fear is a much better teacher than Berlitz. That is why the Jewish people, Mona, have always learned many languages. But did the British in India speak Hindu? Or do the Americans today speak anything at all? Of course not. And now that the Frenchman of Quebec is *maître chez lui*, he too feels that he has the overdog's privilege, which is to remain linguistically ignorant.

"Years ago every French garage mechanic in Montreal used to be able to speak English, but today the rector of the University of Montreal doesn't know how to say 'Hello.' But the French are making a big mistake. Even though they are overdogs locally, they can never be overdogs in the classical sense – not in today's world. Without speaking English they will never be able to function outside this little ghetto they have made for themselves. They have painted themselves into a corner. You just watch what happens when it dawns on them, what they've done to themselves."

For the Anglos, the Nine Good Years came to an abrupt end – or, in Mr. Brophy's phrase, "the balloon went up" – when a survey showed that the bilingual Anglos now had even better jobs, and held even more economic power, than before Separation. The government tried to suppress the results of the survey, but they leaked out, confirming what most of the

French had long suspected, but which was too embarrassing for open discussion. The sad fact was that although every single street name was now in French, and there was not a solitary word in English on a tin of sardines, the big money was still in the pockets of the Anglos.

The news of the survey was greeted with rage by every radical group in Quebec, and they stirred up riots, with much destruction of property. The turmoil went on for three weeks and the government, unwilling to call in the army, seemed unable to restore order. But all the while complex palace intrigues were going on in Quebec City. And one morning President Larocque, always a moderate, resigned and handed over the reins of power to Henri Chartrand, leader of the radical wing of the Parti Québécois.

By afternoon the rioters had gone home and the streets were quiet. The new President declared a state of emergency and sent the members of the National Assembly home. Until the emergency was over, the press would be censored, opposition parties would be illegal, there would be no elections, and all laws would be made by the President and his council. And now, after eleven years, the state of emergency was still in effect, and there was no reason to believe that it would not go on forever.

The first laws promulgated by President Chartrand came the day after his accession to power. They were what the radicals and the intellectuals had long clamoured for – the Linguistic Purity Laws. Under this series of edicts, Anglos could no longer hold positions of importance without passing an examination that would assess the quality of the French they spoke. And Anglos who had thought themselves to be fluent in French soon learned that their French was not quite good enough. The rigours of the examination were almost beyond belief, for the most minuscule grammatical error was now seen as an ominous threat to the survival of Québécois culture.

After failing his examination eleven years ago Mr. Brophy had had to step down as vice-president of Richmond, Foster

and Clark Limited. And, after a period of vocational un-
certainty, he found his present calling as a milkman. Jack
Rosenstein, Mona's father, also failed his examination and immediately ceased being a chartered accountant. Now he too roamed
the streets with a horse and wagon, but unlike Mr. Brophy he
didn't have the security of a job with a milk company; Rosenstein's calling was a more precarious one, as an entrepreneur — a
purchaser and recycler of old rags, bones, and bottles.

As for Mr. Brophy's old company, R.F.C. Limited, it soon
vanished in the wake of the Linguistic Purity Laws. Once it had
occupied a large part of the eleventh floor of the Sun Life
Building, where Paul Pritchard now worked as a farmer, and
here Mr. Brophy would sit in his office, behind a huge desk,
talking on the phone to Aureliano Aguinaga in Caracas. Señor
Aguinaga was the president of Venezuela's biggest chemical
company, and Mr. Brophy would crack jokes with him — in
English — and sell him tons of polymeric plasticizers and ure-
thane catalysts.

The floor where Mr. Brophy once sat at his rosewood desk
was now splendidly green with its abundance of lettuce. There
was Iceberg lettuce and Boston lettuce, Romaine and Butter-
crunch, Deep Heart and Bibb — the finest varieties, in season
and out, for the tables of Quebec's senior army officers and
other gourmets who were high up in the government.

"These credit cards must have been worth a lot," Doreen
Brewster was saying. "What I mean is, if you ran out of money
before payday, could you take your credit card to a pawnshop
and hock it, like it was a watch or a musical instrument?
Would they give you good money for it?"

"Well, to start with, Doreen," said Mr. Brophy, "you didn't
have hundreds of pawnshops in Montreal those days the way
you do now. But putting that aside for a moment, I don't think
you've grasped the basic principle of the credit card. You
see..."

But just then the supper bell rang and the hungry boarders
started trooping down the hall to the dining-room. Mr. Brophy

told Doreen that he would try again, at some future time, to explain to her the wonders of credit in the good old days, before the balloon went up.

In the dining-room, Mrs. MacVicar was waiting for them, sitting at the head of the table. She was a burly, florid woman in her late fifties. She claimed to be a widow, but it was widely believed that her husband had gone over the border as a snow-back, years ago – a refugee not from Quebec but from his wife's despotism and her cooking.

"Mutton stew tonight," Mrs. MacVicar said, her jaunty tone of voice implying that everyone would be pleasantly surprised. But of course for the last few hours everyone had been fully aware of what the menu would be, with the smell of mutton permeating every corner of the house. This greasy odour would be present for two more days, even though there would be no actual mutton in tomorrow night's repeat of the stew, just the lumpy, greyish-brown sauce and the big cubes of potato and turnip. But on the following day, the mutton would make a reappearance, this time served cold, in micrometer-thin slices. It would be accompanied by Mrs. MacVicar's vaunted chutney, which was made mostly of watery mustard and gritty bits of raw cauliflower.

The boarders were passing their plates to the head of the table and Mrs. MacVicar was ladling out the stew from her tureen. Paul and Mona were sitting next to each other and, under the table, his hand sought out hers and held it tenderly. His desire for her body surged within him and he became aware of considerable commotion in his trousers. But, damn it, it wouldn't be tonight. But if not tonight, when? The problem was becoming agonizing.

Meanwhile, the first complaint of the meal was being registered by Colin Armitage. "I don't seem to have any real meat in my stew," he was saying. "It's all sinew and gristle."

"That's exactly what you need – fibre," said Mrs. MacVicar. "If you ate more of the fibre I give you you'd be more regular. But some of us are too lazy to *chew* our food, aren't we?"

"Where's all this fibre?" said Doreen Brewster. "I haven't got any fibre. Mine's all fat. Rubbery fat."

"I'll thank *you*, Miss Brewster, not to come to the supper table in your bathrobe," said Mrs. MacVicar. "You know very well that that's against the rules."

"It's not a bathrobe, it's a *peignoir*."

"And I'll thank you not to bring your roll of toilet tissue into the dining-room. Even if it *is* pink."

"I'd like to know how she can afford pink bum-blotters on *her* salary," Armitage said, in a loud whisper, to Lionel Greenspoon. It was Armitage's revenge for Doreen's not letting him have those extra few minutes in the bathroom earlier that evening.

"Just what do you mean by that remark, Mr. Armitage?" said Spiro Costakis, in a menacing tone. He was poised in his chair, as though about to stand up and hit Armitage.

"Don't get me wrong," Armitage said hastily. "I didn't mean anything, I assure you."

"Apologize to the lady," said Costakis.

"I'm sorry, Doreen," Armitage mumbled. "I apologize."

"I accept your apology," Doreen said haughtily. "But please do not let it occur again."

Paul and Mona exchanged a glance. There had been a suspicion in the house, for the last few days, that Doreen and Costakis had become lovers. This protective attitude of Costakis's seemed to confirm it. Also, pink toilet paper was just the sort of gift Costakis would give to his girlfriend.

"Before I serve the dessert," Mrs. MacVicar was saying, "I must bring up an unpleasant subject. I have reason to believe that something illicit is going on at night in one of the rooms. The guilty parties will know what I mean." She looked straight at Doreen and then at Costakis.

"I have no proof," she continued, "but I have heard certain sounds. You all know that we do not tolerate that sort of thing in this house. As of tonight, no bedroom doors are to be locked from the inside. I may drop in at any time of the night to make sure that nothing is going on."

"Wait a minute," said Paul, "that's unreasonable."

"Why is it unreasonable? Is it reasonable to drag down the reputation of this house?"

"It's an invasion of privacy," said Paul.

"People who are asleep will have nothing to fear," said Mrs. MacVicar. "I shall wear my soft slippers – the fluffy ones – and I shall not wake anyone up. But people who are awake and are doing something will have to start packing their bags immediately."

"Just a minute!" said Spiro Costakis, who again seemed to be very angry. "I want to bring this whole thing out into the open. Do you think you're God, Mrs. MacVicar? Just what the hell is *wrong* with making love? Is there anything more normal in this world than to make love?"

Mona and Paul exchanged another look. Had Costakis been drinking? He was taking a big risk, talking to Mrs. MacVicar that way. He knew very well that in her dictionary the phrase "making love" was an obscenity.

"I will overlook your language this time, Mr. Costakis," said Mrs. MacVicar. "As for what is wrong with – with the thing you refer to, I can only say that it is forbidden by every religion known to mankind – except for people who are married, of course, and no one in this house *is* married."

"That was a hundred years ago," Costakis said. "No religion believes that any more."

"Oh no? Well I happen to go to church, Mr. Costakis, and I don't think you do. I know what is allowed and what is not. And if you talk about many years ago, you should know that the reason we Anglos have lost the position we once had in Quebec is pure and simple – degenerate morals."

Mrs. MacVicar then launched into her lecture about the decline and fall of the Roman Empire. Like all Anglo boarding house keepers she firmly believed that the sole cause of Rome's misfortunes had been the prevalence of extra-marital sex. The decline of the Anglos in Montreal had come about for exactly the same reason, except that it had been hastened by the presence of rock-and-roll music. It was a theory frequently heard from the pulpits of Anglo churches and synagogues.

"We Anglos became animals, especially with that music," Mrs. MacVicar said. "We were animals, but not strong animals. We were weak animals. Animals that were played out."

"Can I ask you a question, Mrs. MacVicar?" said Doreen.

"Yes, Doreen. What is it?"

"How come the French are running this country? They're not declining like the Romans and yet they screw like rabbits."

"You will please leave the table, Miss Brewster," said Mrs. MacVicar. "We simply cannot have that kind of language."

"Now just a minute," said Costakis. "You stay where you are, Doreen. And you answer the question, Mrs. MacVicar. Just tell us how it fits in with your theory – how the Frenchman can be top dog and still he bangs like a mink."

"You will please leave the table, Mr. Costakis."

"How do you explain it, Mrs. MacVicar?" said Doreen. "I'm not talking about French people who are married. I'm talking about young people like us, single people. They don't have to live in dumps like this. They can afford apartments. And you know very well what goes on in those apartments."

"In an apartment you have a private entrance," Costakis explained.

"I will not serve the dessert until Miss Brewster and Mr. Costakis leave the table," said Mrs. MacVicar.

"If they have to leave the table," said Paul Pritchard, "I suggest we all leave. Let's all of us skip the dessert." Under the table Mona's hand gave his an admiring squeeze.

"Not so fast," said Colin Armitage. "Some of us may *want* that dessert. I think the decent thing would be if Doreen and Spiro stopped making such a fuss and just quietly left the table."

"He wants the dessert because he knows it's prunes," said Doreen. "He hopes it'll blast him out of his misery."

"I consider that remark vulgar," said Armitage.

"Oh, come on, Spiro, let's go," said Doreen. Picking up her roll of pink toilet paper, she took Costakis's arm and together they marched out of the dining-room, he glaring at Mrs. Mac-Vicar and she looking straight ahead, her nose in the air.

Mrs. MacVicar went into the kitchen and came back with the dessert. "All's well that ends well," she said, as she started dishing it out. "This way everybody will be able to have an extra prune."

5

After supper, Paul and Mona went out of the boarding house and started walking up Rue Antonio Barrette. It was a street of rundown red-brick houses that had been built, as cheaply as possible, ninety years ago, for working men and their families. The houses looked exhausted with age, as though they might have collapsed long ago and had survived only because they were row houses, leaning wearily against each other and propping each other up. Mrs. MacVicar's establishment consisted of two of these houses, joined together on the inside by a passageway.

"You said you had good news and bad news," said Paul, as they walked. "What's the bad news?"

"I'm not going to get my certificate," said Mona. "And I'm not going to be a designer." She told him what had happened that afternoon in Martineau's office.

"The son of a bitch," said Paul. "But what's your good news?"

"The good news, Paul, is that we don't have to put up with it. Not with Martineau, not with Mrs. MacVicar, not with the mutton stew."

"What do you mean?"

"Let's not talk about it now," said Mona, in a low voice. There was another couple walking behind them, and other people were passing them; they could easily be overheard.

They had come out of the dingy back street where they lived and they were now walking along a busier thoroughfare, Wellington Street. Despite the French name it had been given twenty years ago, this street would always be called Wellington Street by the Anglos. And the neighbourhood would always be called The Point, short for Point St. Charles.

The Point had once been the home of Canada's Irish immigrants. They were the labourers who, in the nineteenth century, built the Victoria Bridge across the St. Lawrence River and pushed the Grand Trunk Railway out into Canada's heartland. They worked in the gloomy factories along the Lachine Canal, making nails and shovels and paint for the new Dominion. In those days, there were more English than French in Montreal and there could even be an Irish mayor, like Jimmy McShane.

The Irish continued to dominate The Point well into the twentieth century, and they made Wellington Street a street with spirit; its weddings, funerals and parades were the liveliest in town. It was a convivial street, busy with the comings and goings of members of the Ancient Order of Hibernians, the United Irish Societies, the Knights of Columbus and the Canadian Legion.

But slowly the factories of The Point became antiquated, and industry moved away. There were fewer and fewer people with jobs and more and more on welfare. By the time Separation came, a large part of The Point was a slum. By the time the Nine Good Years were over, all of it was a slum. It was the very bottom of the barrel, and thus it was the obvious neighbourhood for Anglos to move into, now that they had been rendered desperately poor, as a result of the Linguistic Purity Laws.

By now Wellington Street had completely lost its old spirit. There were still plenty of strollers on a warm evening in May, but they had no spring in their step. They trudged heavily into taverns of the most dismal kind, or into sad little fish-and-chips shops where they ate off greasy newspapers. Those who didn't have enough money in their pockets for a beer or a limp piece of haddock would pass the time by stopping at every pawnshop window, to gaze at the items for sale – broken toasters, rusty

53

harmonicas, second-hand shoes, dust-covered trusses to shore up your hernia.

Hand in hand, Paul and Mona walked along this melancholy street, past the used mattress depot, past the horsemeat butcher's, past the squat, grey building that housed the public baths and the de-lousing station. Finally they reached Marguerite Bourgeoys Park and entered its welcoming darkness.

The last of the lights in the park had long ago been extinguished by Anglo slingshots, and the darkness offered a measure of privacy for the young lovers sitting on the benches, all of them embracing passionately. But every so often a flashlight would snap on, briefly illuminating one of the couples. The flashlights were wielded by muscular men in their forties, volunteer members of the Morality Patrol of the Presbyterian Vigilance League; their mandate was to protect the frayed fabric of Anglo society by making sure that none of the necking and groping degenerated into actual fornication.

Also patrolling the park were a few uniformed members of the Recreation Police. These French officers were not particularly concerned with the possibility of a mass outbreak of coitus; their task was mainly to break up the fist-fights that occasionally flared up when an enraged Anglo youth, suddenly the victim of a flashlight, would leap up and attack a Presbyterian patrolman. The Recreation Police broke up the fights with a good-naturedness seldom seen among Quebec lawmen, for they never ceased to be amused by this continuing spectacle of Anglo masochism.

Paul and Mona walked quickly through the park, to its very end. Here, near the railway tracks, was a solitary bench, partly hidden by a hedge. This was their usual bench and tonight, like most nights, it was unoccupied.

Paul put his arm around her as they sat down and they gazed solemnly into each other's eyes. But she was glad that he made no move to embrace her, for she desperately wanted to talk.

"It all became clear to me," she said. "This afternoon, while

I was coming home. We have to leave this country, Paul. It's as simple as that."

"And where should we go?"

"New York."

"And then what?"

"We lose ourselves in the big city."

"And what do we do for money?"

"We get jobs."

"Without work permits, right?"

"Right. There's snowbacks doing it all the time, aren't there?"

It was true. Some Anglos did manage to find work in the States, without papers. In the cities, they washed dishes or cleaned toilets; in the country they picked fruit; and everywhere they were paid less than the minimum wage. They were constantly being harassed, blackmailed and betrayed. Many were captured and taken back to Quebec; those who avoided capture led furtive lives, on the outskirts of American society.

"In Quebec," said Paul, "we're all poor. In the States, we'd be the *only* ones who were poor. Everybody around us would be well-off. It would be much harder to take."

"Who wants to be rich?" said Mona. "Do you?"

"I don't mean rich, but to have enough money to maintain your self-respect."

"I know what I'd do, Paul, I'd read the theatrical trade papers and I'd see what shows were coming up and I'd submit costume sketches on spec. Eventually I'd get jobs – costumes for extras, work as an assistant, that sort of thing. All under the table, without a work permit. But eventually I'd have enough money to hire a lawyer and try to get papers as an immigrant. Important people in the theatre would know me then and that would help."

As she spoke she was watching his face intently, looking for the enthusiasm she wanted to kindle. But Paul's face showed only that he was troubled and, it seemed to her, that he probably thought she was being totally impractical. Was this really the man for her, she wondered, so solid and reliable? Or did she need someone just a bit less cautious, just a bit more adventurous?

"Tell me," Paul was saying, "have you given up all hope of ever becoming a designer at *l'Atelier*?"

"I told you, I can't get my certificate. And without that I can't be a designer."

"Maybe you could take the examination again. Now that you've failed it twice you know the ropes. Maybe a third time you'd pass."

"I could never pass, Paul," she said. And as they sat in silence, holding hands, Mona felt an unaccustomed resentment toward him; he had managed very nicely to almost snuff out the excitement of her dream. And now he wanted her to try, once again, for that goddam Linguistic Purity Certificate! Bitterly she recalled the last time she had taken the examination, only a month ago, at the headquarters of the *Office pour la défense de la langue de la patrie*.

The three examiners had been sickeningly gallant. One of them had held her chair for her as she sat down and then had gone round to join his fellow inquisitors at the other side of the table. They had started by asking her to conjugate some of the most exasperating of the French irregular verbs and she had done this flawlessly, without a single misstep, not even in the darkest jungles of the imperfect subjunctive. Then they had engaged her in a conversation about the principles of rhetoric and she had been able to converse in fluent French on the differences between zeugma and syllepsis, pleonasm and *périssologie*. Then they had asked her to identify a poem by Emile Nelligan and comment on it; she had done so in an impromptu twenty-minute dissertation, with quotations from apposite verses by Saint-Denys-Garneau. All in French, of course.

"Your grasp of our culture is remarkable," the chief examiner had said. "I only wish my graduate students, whose mother tongue is French, were all as knowledgeable as you."

"Yes indeed," said the second examiner.

"Thank you," said Mona. "I owe it all to my parents, who insisted that I work very hard at my French, from my earliest childhood days."

"That is very commendable," said the third examiner. "But now shall we move on to the pronunciation tests?"

Her heart pounding, Mona accompanied the examiners into the laboratory, where they sat her down in front of a complicated electronic machine. They handed her cards with sentences on them and as she spoke the sentences an oscilloscope flickered and the machine emitted a paper tape with wiggly tracks on it, like an electrocardiogram. After ten minutes of this they turned the apparatus off and the examiners and two white-coated technicians huddled over the tapes. Finally the chief examiner spoke.

"I regret, Miss Rosenstein, that we cannot give you the requisite passing mark," he said. "To anyone's ear, of course, you speak French with a flawless Quebec accent. But science tells us otherwise. Look at these tapes."

And one of the technicians patiently showed her where she had gone wrong. The variance of half a squiggle on the graph, at the spot where she had said *ligne*, showed how the *gn* sound had been prolonged a microsecond too long. This meant that in uttering the word she had raised her upper lip three millimetres higher than was prescribed by the standards of linguistic purity.

The graph showed several other departures from the ideal, involving sounds made by the hard palate, the soft palate and the blade of the tongue. In analyzing Mona's pronunciation of the first *r* in *labourer*, the machine found a small suspicion of a uvular sound rather than a purely dental one. And in pronouncing *fin*, Mona had expelled two cubic centimetres more air through her nose than was permissible.

"Even though the human ear cannot detect these subtle errors," said the chief examiner, "they nevertheless constitute a threat to the survival of Québécois culture. We must be vigilant. Today's tiny variances can grow into tomorrow's gross solecisms. Before long our people would be completely debased, speaking English rather than French. Thus, my dear, I regret that we cannot grant you the Certificate of Linguistic Purity."

And thus, thought Mona, you make sure that I never get a good job, that I continue to provide cheap Anglo labour for the French. She was tempted to say it aloud, but she restrained herself; the Language Police could be very nasty about what it called "insults to the majority culture."

Now, sitting in the park, Mona felt tears coming to her eyes as she thought about the examination. She felt Paul's arm encircling her shoulder, holding her tight, and she knew he shared her distress. It was very comforting; perhaps dear, solid Paul *was* better for her, after all, than somebody more adventurous.

"All right, you're not going to get the certificate," Paul was saying. "But what if they give permission for some theatre in English? There's talk about that, isn't there? You wouldn't need a certificate for that. As far as they're concerned, you'd only be designing Anglo costumes for Anglo actors – a matter of no importance."

She felt a surge of warmth for Paul and she leaned over to kiss him. But suddenly a light was shone into their eyes. It was a Presbyterian patrolman with a flashlight.

Paul leapt to his feet and lunged at the patrolman, but the patrolman stepped aside, laughing.

"I'm going to kill you!" Paul shouted, going for the patrolman again, but another man stepped out of the darkness and grabbed him from behind, pinning his arms.

"Take it easy, son, take it easy," said the patrolman who was holding him. But Paul was writhing and struggling to get free.

Now Mona was on her feet, rushing over to Paul. "Stop it, Paul!" she shouted. "There's two of them and just one of you."

Gradually Paul stopped struggling and the patrolman released him.

"We're just trying to do our job," said the man with the flashlight.

"Some day I'm going to smash your face in," said Paul.

"Sure, sure," said the man. "Meanwhile, just keep your pants buttoned, that's all we ask of you." And the two patrolmen moved away, chuckling.

Paul and Mona sat down again on the bench and sat without talking. Paul was still trembling with rage. Then, suddenly, he put his hand into his coat pocket and brought it out covered with red pulp.

"Oh, Paul!" cried Mona. "Is that blood?"

"No, it's tomatoes. They got crushed."

"*Tomatoes*...?"

"Yes. Chucky and I stole some at work today." And he told her how they had done it. The story delighted Mona and she threw her arms around him and smothered him with kisses. As she did this it suddenly occurred to her that she really didn't know Paul very well.

She had never seen him in a rage before and it seemed out of keeping with the Paul she knew. And this boldness in stealing the tomatoes was yet another unexpected side of his character. No, she surely did not know him well. She didn't know, for instance, just what his hopes and dreams for the future were, or if he really had any at all. In the months they had been together all she had learned was that he was interested in agriculture. Perhaps that was because he had volunteered very little information about himself; they had always talked about *her* ambitions. Now she felt a sudden pang of guilt about that.

"What is it *you* want to do, Paul?" she said, softly. "For the future, I mean. You've never really told me."

"I'd like to be a farmer," said Paul. "Not in the Sun Life Building but on a real farm, in the country. A farm of my own. I suppose I've never discussed it because I didn't think a theatrical designer would see much of a future on a farm."

They sat in silence. What he had just said could be interpreted as having to do with marriage, or with some permanent commitment, and the idea made Mona uncomfortable. Now she wondered how to phrase her next question. She wanted to pursue the matter of Paul's ambitions, but she didn't want the conversation to drift in the direction of wedding bells.

"I don't feel right about leaving Quebec," Paul was saying. "My family has lived here for six generations."

"But there's no future here, is there?"

"There are still some Anglo farmers in the Eastern Townships. In fact I have an uncle down there who has a small farm. I've often thought he might take me on as a partner. He's getting pretty old and I could do all the work for him."

"What does *he* say to that?"

"Well, I've never discussed it with him."

"Oh? How come?"

"Well, he's a very eccentric old chap. Hates the rest of the family. Refuses to talk to us, as a matter of fact. He's a sort of a hermit."

"So your dreams are as impractical as mine," said Mona.

"Yes, I guess so," said Paul.

She reached over and stroked his cheek tenderly and he looked at her glumly.

"But life on a farm can be marvellous, you know," he said.

"In Quebec?" she said. "With all the regulations? With the government looking over your shoulder all day and all night?"

"Yes, that's not too good."

"I can just see you on your farm, Paul. Everything's going fine and then out of the blue the Veterinary Police come along and put you in jail. You know why?"

"No, why?"

"Because you've been giving commands to your sheepdog in English, that's why."

"Well," said Paul, as they got up to leave the park, "I guess I'd just have to be very careful about things like that." And he *would* have to be careful. The law was very clear on that particular point. All animals, sheepdogs included, were considered to be part of *le patrimoine national* and for them too the language of work had to be French.

6

"I hear some people have been going out to Bisaillon Park," said Paul. "Have you ever been out there?"

"No," said Chucky Dwyer, "I'm not even too sure I know where it is."

"It's way out at the end of Boulevard Lise Payette. Practically in the country."

"That's one hell of a bicycle trip."

"They say there's absolutely no Morality Patrol out there at all."

"Well, if there isn't I'm sure they'll get around to it eventually."

"They say it's very quiet at night," said Paul. "Lots of tall grass and bushes. No lights or anything like that."

"Like in the old joke, eh?" said Chucky. "Farmer Brown says, 'I don't know what to do, I keep finding these condoms in my haystack.' And Farmer Jones says, 'You think *you've* got problems? Why, on a hot summer night I've had up to fifty acres of flax fucked flat.'"

Chucky Dwyer laughed heartily at his own joke, but Paul could manage only a weak smile. Chucky, who worked on the nineteenth floor of the farm, in carrots and parsnips, had suggested that they have lunch outdoors, taking advantage of the warm May sunshine. So they were now sitting in Place Lévesque, which had once been known as Dominion Square, eating their sandwiches and watching the girls go by.

For today's lunch, Mrs. MacVicar had supplied Paul with

61

two cold mutton sandwiches and an aged, wrinkled apple. The sandwiches were pitifully thin and the mutton was by now so desiccated that it tasted like sand, and its heavy marbling of cold fat was reminiscent of soap. By contrast, Chucky's lunch was a banquet – two sandwiches made with plump rolls, thickly buttered and generously filled, one with Cheddar cheese and the other with expensive salami. To round out the meal, Chucky's landlady, Mrs. Standish, had given him a portion of canned peaches in a small plastic container, an incredible delicacy. It was not for nothing that there was a long waiting list of people who wanted to get into Mrs. Standish's boarding house.

"I guess the ground would still be pretty wet, this time of year," Paul said. "Out at Bisaillon Park, I mean. After all the snow we had this winter."

"Probably would be," said Chucky. "Like the little bird said, eh, 'Too wet to woo.'" Again Chucky laughed heartily.

It was Paul who had brought up the old question of where a chap could take his girlfriend at night, to make love. He was trying to make it sound as though he was discussing the problem in the abstract, as just another burden the Anglos had to bear. He didn't want Chucky to know how urgently personal the problem had become. But he had a growing sense of apprehension, a feeling of doom, about his relationship with Mona. If they didn't make love soon, if they didn't progress to the next logical step in their passion, it might all fall apart. Already they seemed to be losing some of their closeness; he had felt that the other night, when she had suggested running away to the States.

"It's really an injustice, isn't it?" said Paul. "I mean when Anglos have to take their girls into grass that's soaking wet."

"I don't want to be personal," said Chucky, "but you sound pretty desperate."

"Who? Me?" said Paul.

"Yes, you."

Paul pursed his lips, thoughtfully. But the pressure was too much and he suddenly found himself blurting it all out: "Goddam it, Chucky, I'm at my wits' end! I'm going out of my mind! I may go crazy!"

"That's rough, fella," said Chucky. "That's really rough."

"It's so goddam unfair! We both – we both want it so badly."

"And there's nothing doing where you live? You can't get rid of your roommate?"

"It's not just that any more. It's that old bitch Mrs. MacVicar. She now pads around at night looking into the rooms. Checking that nobody's doing it."

"Like I always said, it's not the French who're our enemies, it's our *own* damn people."

"I guess I'll just have to make a trip out there," said Paul. "Test the grass and see for myself if it's wet."

"Don't let me discourage you," said Chucky, "but I always hate the thought of Anglos doing it in the bushes."

"What do you mean?"

"Well, a race of people can go into decline, like the Anglos, and still maintain some of their pride. But once they start copulating in the bushes, they've really sunk low. The next thing you know, it's back to the loin-cloth and the spear."

"I never thought of it that way."

"But maybe that's the tragedy of the Anglo," said Chucky. "What's the alternative for a healthy young guy? He either heads out for the tall grass country, like your Bisaillon Park, or he stays home and pulls his wire."

Paul watched glumly as Chucky started eating his canned peaches. They were halves of peaches, voluptuously smooth, in heavy syrup.

"God, when I think of it, it makes me shudder," said Chucky. "All those poor buggers lying in bed, beating their meat all night long. And the girls tickling their twats with long feathers. If it goes on much longer, the whole Anglo race is going to go blind."

Paul attempted a laugh, but the subject was too disturbing. He himself seemed to be doing it much more often these days than ever before. The nightly visions of Mona's writhing body

63

were becoming ever more lurid, and the struggle he always had with himself, trying to desist, was becoming ever more perfunctory.

Could it really be harmless? At school the boys used to reassure each other that "modern medical science" had conclusively proven that there was no hazard whatever to one's health, that the practice might even be beneficial. But the booklet *Personal Standards for You*, now being distributed to young people by the Presbyterian Vigilance League, had a far more alarming point of view. Whom could one believe?

"This whole sex thing is a tragedy," Chucky was saying, "but it's one thing we can't blame on the French. We've bloody well brought it on ourselves."

"I don't agree with you," said Paul. "If the French paid us decent wages a lot of our problems would be solved. All we need is some money in our pockets."

"That's a cop-out. If you're smart you can solve a lot of problems *without* money."

Paul looked at him, suddenly wondering what Chucky himself did to ease the torment. Did Chucky always live by his own lofty precepts? Did he always manage to avoid the degradation of the bushes, or the tall grass? Did he never find that he simply *had* to take himself in hand?

"How about you, Chucky?" Paul said. "How do you manage with this sex thing? Or is that a personal question?"

"Well," said Chucky, "I have to admit that I'm not suffering too much these days."

"But where do you go? Does Mrs. Standish let everybody do it in their room?"

"Not on your life, Buster. Mrs. Standish is just as strict as Mrs. MacVicar. Even stricter."

"Then what do you do?"

"I bang Mrs. Standish, that's what I do."

Paul stared at Chucky. Could this incredible thing be true? It was almost beyond imagining.

"You're kidding me, aren't you?" said Paul.

"It's the honest truth," said Chucky. "You don't think Mrs. Standish prepares a lunch like this for *all* the boarders, do you? If she did she'd be bankrupt in a week." With a wink at Paul, he finished the last spoonful of thick peach syrup and threw the little plastic container over his shoulder.

Reluctantly, Paul decided that it must be true. But how could there be so much injustice in the world? He vividly remembered meeting Mrs. Standish one night while visiting Chucky for a game of chess. She was a very handsome widow in her early forties. She had been in and out of the parlour all evening and her splendid behind, in tight pink slacks, had been so distracting that it cost Paul his queen, a bishop and at least two pawns.

"How about taking a walk?" Chucky Dwyer was saying. "There's something I want to pick up at Eaton's."

"All right," said Paul, and they got to their feet and moved off in the direction of Rue Ste. Catherine.

Eaton's was still the city's biggest department store, even though only the ground floor was still in use; the other eight floors had long ago been closed for lack of merchandise. It was still called Eaton's by the Anglos, although its name was now Le Comptoir National. Like all large corporations, this store had been nationalized soon after the end of the Nine Good Years, when Quebec became a socialist state. Only the smallest businesses could now be privately owned, and these enterprises were strictly controlled, lest they become too profitable and lead to a recrudescence of capitalism. Permits to own them were granted only to the most trustworthy persons, such as relatives of high government officials.

"What are you buying?" asked Paul, as they entered Le Comptoir National.

"A little present for Mrs. Standish," said Chucky. "Nothing too expensive, mind you."

In the leather goods department, Chucky examined some massive and rather crude handbags imported from Soviet Turkestan. But they were seventy-five piastres each – far too costly.

There were some goatskin slippers from Bulgaria, but these too were out of Chucky's price range. They moved on to the beauty products department, where they examined some toiletries from Romania.

Much of the merchandise in Le Comptoir National was imported from Communist countries, bought with rubles that Quebec earned by selling hydroelectric power to the Soviet Union. The Russians had laid a cable under the Arctic Ocean, from James Bay to Leningrad, and the enormous wattage that travelled through it every day provided Quebec with its principal source of foreign exchange.

"This Communist junk is too bloody expensive," said Chucky, putting down a flask of Romanian bath salts. "Let's go over there and look at the homemade stuff."

They crossed the store to a large section at the far end which bore a sign saying *Fabrication Québécoise*. Here there was a surprising variety of items and all of them – including vacuum cleaners and electric can-openers – were painstakingly hand made. In the new Quebec, very few items were mass produced and there were no assembly lines.

Manufacturing, in the industrial sense of the word, had petered out after Separation, largely as a result of Quebec's policy of paying its workers the highest minimum wage in the western world and accepting from them, in return, the lowest productivity. After all, it made no sense to produce your own refrigerators and light bulbs and toothbrushes when you could import them at half the price from North Korea.

But this economic policy had a few disadvantages, from the consumer's point of view. Not the least of these was the erratic nature of the Communists' export offerings. One year there would be all the refrigerators anyone would want, but then, for the next four years, there would be none at all. In recent years there had been lots of wicker baby carriages and ornamental camel bells, but few of the electrical appliances that people wanted so badly. Thus Quebec artisans were starting to make household implements by hand, just as their ancestors had in the seventeenth century. But now it was vacuum cleaners rather than spinning wheels, toasters rather than rocking chairs.

The government spoke proudly of the revival of age-old crafts and it hailed the disappearance of hundreds of smoke-spewing factories as a great boon to public health. "Quebec is in the forefront once again," said the President, "leading the nations of the world into a new epoch for mankind, the Post-Industrial Age."

But the new age had its drawbacks, among them the fact that hand-crafted refrigerators were so expensive that only high government officials could afford to buy them. And most of the small appliances that Paul and Chucky were now examining would cost them several months' wages. But there were one or two bargains.

"How about this?" said Paul, holding up a highly-ornamented, hand-tooled bicycle pump.

"Too practical," said Chucky. "I need something more romantic."

He found it in the artificial flowers department – a bouquet of daffodils made of brightly-coloured plastic. It came from Albania and was on sale for only six piastres and fifteen centimes.

"This will really hit the spot," Chucky said, as they left the store. "When Mrs. Standish gets carried away she likes to do a little dance in the bedroom with a flower in her mouth. Naked, of course."

As they walked back to work, Paul became alarmed at the intensity of the envy he was feeling. It had been growing steadily, from the moment Chucky had unwrapped his first luncheon sandwich, the one that was stuffed with a reckless amount of costly salami. Now the vision of Mrs. Standish doing her lascivious dance was the last straw.

"Let's make a little detour here, do you mind?" said Chucky, as they reached Rue Claude Morin. "It's only a block out of our way. There's something up there I'd like to have a look at."

They walked up the street toward the large building that housed part of the Ministry of Culture. There had been an explosion here, a big one that had blown in part of the building's façade. Near the hole a message had been painted, in huge red letters – FREE THE ANGLOS. The Anglo Liberation Army had struck again, during the night.

"I heard about it this morning, at work," Chucky said.

"That must have taken a lot of dynamite," Paul said.

They wanted to look more closely into the hole, but the area was roped off and policemen were hastening people along, so that no crowd could form. Meanwhile workmen were putting up their ladders to sandblast, paint over, or somehow obliterate the A.L.A.'s slogan. The words were not only seditious, they were in a language other than French, which was strictly prohibited.

"'Free the Anglos,'" Chucky said. "What idiots! What a hopeless cause."

"I don't know, Chucky," said Paul. "Maybe it isn't so hopeless."

"Are you kidding?"

The aims of the Anglo Liberation Army were certainly visionary and perhaps quixotic. They called for total separation from Quebec and the creation of an independent Angloland. This would take in the western half of the Island of Montreal, traditional home of the urban Anglos, and part of the Eastern Townships, traditional home of the rural Anglos. The old Autoroute that linked the two areas would become a demilitarized corridor.

The name Angloland was provisional; one faction in the A.L.A. wanted to call it New Canada. But whatever its name, its advocates argued that it would be a perfectly viable country. Its area would be much bigger than Singapore or Mauritius or Malta or several other sovereign states. In fact, its size would be equal to the *combined* area of six European countries: Luxembourg, Liechtenstein, Vatican City, San Marino, Monaco, and Andorra. And its population would be twice as big as the combined population of those six sovereign states.

Unlike Quebec, Angloland would enjoy good relations with the United States, and this would lead to trade and prosperity. But pride was more important than mere prosperity; this would be a country where Anglos could work in their own language, develop their own culture, and walk with their heads held high.

But Chucky Dwyer didn't seem to subscribe to this vision. "This sort of thing," he said, gesturing at the bomb hole, "is the worst thing that could happen to the Anglos at this point in time."

"I'm not too sure about that," said Paul. "Don't you think it draws attention to injustice?"

"Sure. And how does the government respond? It punishes the whole community for the acts of a handful of idiots. Next month, for the twentieth anniversary celebrations, the French are getting twenty-one holidays and Anglos are only getting nine. Why? The government doesn't come right out and say it, but it's because there's been far too many bombings."

"The guys who are doing the bombing are taking a hell of a risk," said Paul. "They may be wrong, but they think it's their patriotic duty. You've got to respect that."

"Bullshit, pure bullshit. They're not patriots, they're neurotics. Nothing personal, Paul, but these are probably guys who can't get laid. They're mad as hell, so they throw some bombs – and they call it patriotism."

"According to your theory," said Paul, "the Anglos are blaming everything on the French when we ourselves cause a lot of our own problems. Is that it?"

"Exactly. When you admit that to yourself, you're starting to grow up."

"Well, I'm not admitting it. I still believe that if the Anglos have sex problems – let's just use that as an example of a problem – it wouldn't exist if we had a bit more money. Then we could live in apartments and we wouldn't have to put up with the rules and regulations of Mrs. MacVicar and the morality squad. But we don't have money because we can't get better jobs and we can't get better jobs because the goddam French want to keep us as hewers of wood and drawers of water."

"Where have I heard that song before?" said Chucky. "As soon as you and all the other Anglos stop believing it you'll be on the road to maturity."

"Come to think of it," said Paul, "you seem to have changed your tune, Chucky. Changed it radically. I remember when you used to curse the French so loud I was worried we might get arrested."

"I still curse them. But I don't blame all my troubles on them. Maturity begins when you accept responsibility. Then you can start doing something about your problems."

But, as they walked on, Paul wondered whether the only solution to the problems of the Anglos wasn't what the A.L.A. advocated – a sovereign and independent Angloland, or New Canada. Paul preferred New Canada as a name for a country; Angloland sounded a bit like a dignified amusement park.

The fertile fields of the Eastern Townships would be part of New Canada, and here Paul would have his farm. It would be a very modern, progressive farm, and Paul would have time to enter politics. He would be a Member of Parliament – Paul Pritchard, Member for South Stukely.

A farm on the shores of beautiful Brome Lake ... New Canada would be prosperous and people would have automobiles, running on gasoline. Montreal would be only ninety minutes away from Brome Lake, not two days by bicycle. It would be easy for Mona to go into town whenever they needed her at the theatre; but she would do most of her work – her designing, her sketches – right there on the farm, in her own studio, a lovely little belvedere looking out on the lake. Paul would build it for her with his own hands. For Mona. Mrs. Mona Pritchard. His wife. The thought of marriage had flitted through his head before, but it had never really taken root. But now, he realized, it had suddenly become deeply embedded. It was at the centre of his dream.

"Tell me, Chucky," he said, "wouldn't you like to live in

your own country, in Angloland, or New Canada or whatever they'd call it?"

"Sure I would," said Chucky. "But I'm not going to waste any time thinking about it, because it's totally impossible."

They had reached the Sun Life Building and they were walking up the broad granite steps. They went through the fluted Corinthian columns into the lobby and crossed to the elevators. Paul pressed the button and, as they waited, he looked out into the lobby, marvelling, as he always did, at its beauty – its walls of rose-coloured marble from Italy and its ornamental columns of rare green syenite, standing on bases of black marble from Belgium.

As they waited for an elevator, Officer Poirier of the Agricultural Police came up to them.

"*Sont encore en panne*," he said, nodding to the elevators.

"Oh, shit," said Chucky. "Not again!" And they started to climb the stairs. Paul had eighteen floors to go to reach his celery and his Snowball cauliflowers. Chucky had nineteen, to his carrots and his parsnips.

* * *

"I want to talk to you," Chucky said to Paul, a few days later, as they were leaving work. Instead of going to the bicycle rack they went across the street to Place Lévesque, where they found an isolated bench.

"I want you to know," said Chucky, "that I'm a member of the Anglo Liberation Army. I have been for more than a year. The reason I wanted to look at that bomb damage the other day was because I was one of the guys who planted the bomb."

"You're kidding," said Paul.

"No, I'm not. If you want to know why I was denouncing the A.L.A. the other day it's because I was testing you. I wanted to see if you were angry – angry enough to join us. We need recruits."

There was a silence and then Paul said, "It would mean planting bombs, is that right?"

71

"Yes," said Chucky, "and a few other things I can't tell you about right now."

There was another silence and then Paul said, "Yes, I want to join."

"I don't have to tell you it's extremely dangerous."

"I know that."

Chucky extended his hand and Paul shook it.

"I belong to the General Wolfe Cell," said Chucky. "That'll be your cell too. I'll take you to our meeting on Thursday night."

"What's a cell?" said Paul.

"It's a small, self-sufficient unit. The organization is made up of a number of cells."

Paul's heart was pounding. He realized, suddenly, that this was what he had wanted all along, without knowing it – a way to correct the injustice that he saw all around him. And in the last minute or two, by making his commitment, he felt he had become a different person. And Chucky was different too. Looking at him now, Paul saw a serious, purposeful young man – not the superficial Chucky of old, living only for a thick sandwich and a roll in the hay.

"The other day," said Paul, "you said it was wrong to blame our problems on the French. You don't really believe that, do you?"

"I believe the exact opposite," said Chucky. "Unless a man has freedom, no part of his life can be any good."

"How many people are there in this cell, Chucky?"

"You'll learn that in due time. I should warn you, when I take you to your first meeting, don't ask too many questions. Just listen to everything that's said and you'll gradually learn what you have to know. The policy is for nobody to know more than they have to."

"In case they're captured and interrogated?"

"That's right," said Chucky.

They sat in silence, watching some girls crossing the park. There were three of them, all brunettes. They must be French

72

girls, Paul thought. They were dressed with flair and they walked with that extra bit of bounce that so few Anglo girls had. You certainly wouldn't want to throw bombs at bouncy girls like these three beauties. But surely the General Wolfe Cell would never require you to do that.

"One more thing," Chucky said. "You must never talk about being a member – not to anyone. Nobody can be trusted, absolutely nobody."

"I understand that, Chucky."

"Remember, if you blab you'll be putting other people's lives in danger, not just your own."

"You have my word of honour," said Paul. "Total silence."

"Good," said Chucky. "And remember, that goes especially for your girlfriend. You mustn't ever tell Mona about this."

7

Was Cathy finally becoming a human being? Mona found herself giving serious consideration to this possibility as she sat at her sewing machine at *l'Atelier*, stitching together white smocks to be worn by the Patriotic Artists at the Proclamation of Sovereignty pageant.

If Cathy Burton, Mona's roommate, *was* becoming human, it would make life much more agreeable for Mona. Up until now, Cathy had been consistently unbearable. She left traces of her vivid makeup all over the room and her clothes, most of which desperately needed laundering, were usually strewn over Mona's bed as well as her own.

But Cathy's personality was even worse than her litter. Her conversation consisted entirely of complaints, and her governing emotion, Mona suspected, was envy. Like almost all other boarding house roommates, Mona and Cathy had not chosen each other; when Mona had come to live in the house, Mrs. MacVicar had simply assigned her to the vacant bed in Cathy's room. In Montreal there was a chronic shortage of rooms that Anglos could afford, so you accepted whatever was offered to you.

Mona had tried to give Cathy hints about how to improve her appearance, but Cathy seemed to find this insulting. Mona tried to suggest that Cathy not spend so much time lying in bed, but Cathy was not prepared to even consider this. And Mona's occasional pleas to have the room to herself were always turned down.

But this morning things seemed to have changed. Cathy had

been out of bed before Mona and had spent at least five minutes tidying up. She applied less of the trashy Hungarian makeup to her face than she usually did and she even managed a smile.

"Would you like to have the room to yourself tonight?" she said.

"I'd love that," said Mona.

"All right," said Cathy. "I won't be home until midnight." And she proceeded to ask Mona's opinion about a green blouse that she had produced from her bottom drawer. It could only mean that Cathy had found a boyfriend – or a potential boyfriend. Mona fervently hoped this was the case.

Now, as she stitched the Parti Québécois emblem to the smocks of the Patriotic Artists, Mona wondered just how it would feel to be in Paul's arms, their naked bodies locked together. Tonight was surely going to be *the* night. Not only was Cathy going to be out, but, as it was Thursday, Mrs. MacVicar would be at her regular meeting of the Ladies' Auxiliary of the Presbyterian volunteers. At these meetings the discussions about the depravity of young Anglos were so extensive that the proceedings never terminated before 11:00 P.M.

Yes, tonight would be the night. Paul had said that he would be busy, playing chess with Chucky Dwyer or something, but it would be easy for him to cancel that. Immediately after supper, as soon as Mrs. MacVicar went out the door, they would go up to her room. And Paul would become the second man ever to sleep with Mona. Would he be the last? She wondered about that. Certainly the last for a long, long time. For she was sure that after they had become lovingly familiar with every detail of each other's body, Paul would gladly give up his pipe dream of a farm in the Eastern Townships. Instead, he would be ready for the grand adventure – across the border, through the blizzard, and down to New York.

"Ah, Mademoiselle Rosenstein. With the lovely trace of a smile on her lips and a faraway look in her eyes."

It was the director of *l'Atelier*, the swinish Rodrigue Martineau, who had come up from behind and was now standing in front of her sewing machine.

"How are you today, my dear?" he said.

"I'm fine, thanks."

"You look better than fine. You must be in love. Is that the case?"

Mona couldn't decide which would be the better answer, yes or no, so she said nothing.

"So you are *not* in love," said Martineau. "So much the better. Tell me, do you happen to know a girl called Joyce Latimer, the Anglo girl who works for Gaston Trepanier?"

"Yes, I know her," said Mona. Joyce was an assistant prop girl, doing the most menial of tasks for Trepanier's organization, which was in charge of procuring props for the film industry.

"Has Joyce told you her good fortune?" said Martineau.

"No, I haven't seen her for a while."

"Well, as you know, Joyce is not nearly as talented as you are. And yet Gaston Trepanier has been able to obtain a Certificate of Linguistic Purity for her. It happened only yesterday. Now Joyce will be able to advance very rapidly in her field of endeavour. To say nothing of a better salary. What do you think of that?"

"It makes me sick," said Mona, the words escaping from her before she could stop them.

"Sick with envy?" said Martineau. "Surely that need not be. As you know, I can help you in the same way that Gaston Trepanier has helped Joyce. In fact this very weekend. Does that appeal to you?"

"No, it doesn't," said Mona, determined to keep her voice flat and totally without emotion.

"Ah, you are occupied this weekend," said Martineau. "That is my great misfortune. However I shall ask you again." And with a broad smile he moved off across the big sewing-room.

Mona suddenly felt as though she were suffocating and she

76

got up and went to the window, which was just behind her machine. She breathed deeply as she looked up at the greenery of Mount Royal and then down into the street, where students were going from one university building to another. As she watched them, Mona wished she were down there, using her brain, rather than up here, chained to a sewing machine.

The seamstresses worked in a huge room on the fifth floor of an imposing structure that had once been the McIntyre Medical Sciences Building of McGill University. Here, in the old days, men in white coats had peered through electron microscopes at diseased human tissue, and had tried to chase viruses with ultrasonic beams. But for years now the building had housed more cheerful pursuits – not only the work of *l'Atelier* but also that of the nation's best set designers, prop men, make-up artists and puppet masters.

The medical research centre had been one of the first of McGill's buildings to undergo a metamorphosis after Separation. And, a few years later, McGill itself had ceased to exist. Since 1821 it had been a bastion of the Anglo elite, but now its leafy campus and its historic buildings had become the Université Maurice Duplessis, named after the great advocate of Quebec's autonomy.

It had been hoped that Montreal's Maurice Duplessis University would rival Moscow's Patrice Lumumba University in attracting students from the Third World, particularly from the French-speaking African countries. But few of these students ever showed up, for now that Quebec had entered the Post-Industrial Age many Africans considered Quebec itself to be part of the Third World, having pulled itself *down* by its own bootstraps rather than up. So French-speaking students from Mali and Togo and Upper Volta who wanted to learn engineering went to the University of Dakar, in Senegal, a country that was rapidly becoming industrialized. Other French-speaking students, from Benin, Gabon and Chad, went to universities in Boston or Sheffield or Toronto, where they could learn English.

77

But if the Université Maurice Duplessis failed to find an international role it soon found a national one. It became a centre not only for the theatrical arts but also for the social sciences. Each year it supplied Quebec with thousands of newly-graduated sociologists, all of them eager to join in the task of measuring and calibrating every aspect of human activity in the young republic.

"Mona, are you day-dreaming again?" Madame Tousignant, the sewing-room supervisor, had come up to Mona, who was still standing and looking out the window.

"Sorry," said Mona. "I just needed a bit of air."

"We're behind schedule," said Madame Tousignant, thrusting some patches of cloth at Mona. "These should have been put on yesterday."

"What are they?" said Mona, taking the patches and going back to her machine.

"They're chevrons. For the Allegorical Fishermen. Don't you remember?"

"I think you're wrong. Aren't the chevrons for the Patriotic Artists?"

"Oh, my God, are they?" Madame Tousignant hastily consulted her notebook and saw that Mona was right. "We have to be more careful," she said, irritably, and went rushing across the room, shouting instructions to the girl who was about to start sewing the allegorical moneybags for the Anglo Imperialists. Although it was Madame Tousignant's job to maintain order, there was no doubt that she herself unleashed most of the waves of panic that frequently surged through the sewing-room.

Sitting down at her machine, Mona consulted the instruction sheet that would tell her just how to sew the chevrons to the sleeves of the Patriotic Artists. This had been very carefully worked out, at the highest level, and no mistakes would be tolerated.

The lowest rank – one small V-shaped stripe – meant, quite simply, that the wearer was an Artist. Two small stripes denoted Promising Artist and three meant Important Artist. One large stripe, fringed in scarlet, labelled the wearer as a Leading Artist, and two such stripes meant he was a Master Artist. The highest rank – three very large stripes fringed in scarlet *and* gold – meant that the wearer was truly illustrious, a Creator of the Future Heritage of Quebec.

When the Ministry of Culture introduced this ranking system a few years earlier, almost everyone had greeted it with hearty approval. For the public, the little chevrons embossed in the lower right-hand corner of every Quebec painting would provide invaluable aid in assessing the significance of that particular work. No longer would art be "understood" only by a handful of experts, speaking an obscure jargon.

As the government explained it, this elitism on the part of the experts, this paternalism, had been very important to the strategy of the Anglo colonizers. And now it would be eliminated. And while a few artists grumbled privately about "regimentation," they all endorsed the philosophy behind the scheme. As the president of the National Syndicate of Cultural Workers put it, "Nothing in the world of the Québécois artist can ever take precedence over the struggle to eradicate the colonial mentality."

The ranking of artists was only one aspect of the government's sweeping plans to rationalize the life of the country, to create order where there had been anarchy in the Colonial Era. The time had come to tidy things up – in the French tradition. It was time for Cartesian logic, for ranking things the way Diderot would have ranked them. It was time for codification.

No longer would the Québécois people be oppressed by alien ways of doing things. No longer would they be bewildered by Anglo pragmatism, eclecticism, common law, rule by precedent, entrenchment of usage, *ad hoc* solutions and *a posteriori* thinking. These were the arcane cultural and legislative tools of an in-group – of clubmen, of colonizers who could justify every self-serving injustice by reference to a code that was not even codified.

It was time to recall that the logic of Descartes was one of the glories of western civilization. And here in Quebec that ancient French passion for logical thinking could soar to new heights, thanks to modern tools like the computer – and the data that was constantly being gathered for it by sixty thousand graduate sociologists.

Mona finished sewing the chevrons to the smocks of the Patriotic Artists and looked up from her machine. There was a commotion going on around the workbench of Lisette, one of the youngest seamstresses. Several of the other girls were standing around, looking on, as Madame Tousignant shouted at Lisette and brandished a pair of men's trousers.

"Idiot!" Madame Tousignant was screaming. "I can't believe you can be such an idiot! Perhaps it is sabotage. We will see what Monsieur Martineau says about this!" She marched off toward the director's office, taking the trousers with her. Lisette started crying and one of the girls put her arm around her to comfort her.

Mona got up and went over to join the group. "What's the matter?" she said.

"Lisette made a terrible mistake," said Cecile, one of the seamstresses.

"What did she do?" said Mona.

"The pants," said Cecile. "She made them all like this."

Cecile handed a pair of trousers to Mona, who examined them. They were the trousers to be worn by the Founding Fathers in the Proclamation of Sovereignty pageant. They were made of expensive blue worsted and they looked perfect in every detail.

"You don't notice something?" said Cecile.

"No, they look fine."

"Look at the fly."

But this part, the most complex task in pants making, also looked fine to Mona.

"She should have known better," said Cecile. "She made the right flap close over the left flap."

Of course. Mona hadn't noticed. But the access to a man's zipper is always from the right. Thus the left fly flap always closes over the right one.

"Why does it matter?" said Mona. "Nobody will notice, from a distance."

"Madame Tousignant thinks it's *very* important," said Cecile. "And the pants have to be ready first thing tomorrow morning. We may have to remake them all, which means everybody will have to work tonight, maybe till midnight."

Work tonight? Mona felt a pang of alarm. Tonight was to be *the* night with Paul. When would there be another opportunity, with Cathy out of the room and Mrs. MacVicar out of the house? Mona watched anxiously as Madame Tousignant came striding across the room with Martineau, talking heatedly to him and waving the pants.

"This is the girl that did it – Lisette Latraverse," Madame Tousignant said to him when they reached the scene of the crime. "She has no excuse."

"Ah, Lisette," said Martineau. "I have noticed you but I have not had the pleasure of meeting you."

But Lisette, who was sobbing convulsively, would not look up. She was only seventeen, a wistful blonde beauty with a splendid figure.

"There, there, Lisette," said Martineau. "It is not the end of the world. Here, wipe your tears away." And he handed her a cream-coloured silk handkerchief, richly embroidered with his initials.

Lisette mopped at her eyes and looked up, attempting a brave little smile. All the women in the sewing-room had now left their machines and were standing in a semi-circle around Lisette's workbench.

"I think we have to remake all these pants," said Madame Tousignant. "I really think we must."

"Would they be finished by morning?" said Martineau. As he spoke he patted Lisette lightly on the shoulder, to comfort her.

"We could finish them if everybody worked until midnight," said Madame Tousignant.

The situation, Mona felt, was now becoming very dangerous. She would have to intervene.

"Does it really matter?" Mona said. "I mean, nobody in the audience will notice, from a distance, will they?"

"Ah, the spirited Mademoiselle Rosenstein," said Martineau. "What do you say to that, Madame Tousignant?"

"I think it does matter. Very much," said Madame Tousignant.

"Please explain to me why," said Martineau, all the time looking down at Lisette, who had now stopped weeping.

"These pants will be worn by some of our greatest actors," said Madame Tousignant. "And...uh...actors always go to make pee-pee before a performance, do they not?"

"Yes," said Martineau. "It is a very sensible precaution."

"Well," said Madame Tousignant, "say one of our leading actors, say Jacques Poulin–who is playing the part of one of the greatest of our Founding Fathers, Dr. Camille Laurin–say Jacques Poulin is standing in the men's room just before the performance and he puts his hand down and cannot...uh... cannot find it. I mean cannot get it open. Could this not have a very bad psychological effect?"

There was a titter from the seamstresses and one of them, Marie-Claire, said, "Poor Jacques. He will think someone has stolen his sausage."

The seamstresses roared with laughter and Mona noticed that Martineau was grinning broadly and winking at Lisette. Perhaps things would work out after all.

"I don't think this is funny," said Madame Tousignant. "If the Anglo terrorists themselves tried to sabotage this pageant they couldn't think of a better way. Can't you see them, our Founding Fathers, coming on stage wearing these pants? Lévesque, Laurin, Morin, Parizeau, and all the others. The audience applauds them wildly, but they have just been to the men's room and, even though they may be fine actors, they cannot help but look slightly preoccupied. One or two of them even look worried and the audience wonders what emotion they are trying to convey. Can it be that some of the Founding Fathers are wondering whether Separation was not a mistake after all?"

Madame Tousignant spoke with great conviction and Mona was dismayed to see the smile slowly leaving Martineau's face. Yes, they would be working until midnight. But just then Lisette, whose tears were now totally dry, spoke up unexpectedly.

"I suppose I am fired?" she said in a small voice.

"You most certainly are," said Madame Tousignant.

"In that case, *I* won't be working until midnight," said Lisette, with surprising boldness. She stood up and reached for her handbag. Then she opened her drawer and took some things out to put into the handbag. As she did so, her large and unconfined breasts moved considerably under the thin fabric of her blouse. Mona saw Martineau's eyes widen.

"Now just a minute," said Martineau, putting his hand on Lisette's arm. "You are not fired. Not necessarily."

"In that case," said Madame Tousignant, grim-lipped, "Lisette will sit down at her machine and start remaking one pair of pants. I will distribute the other pairs to the other girls. If we start immediately we can finish by midnight. But not if we stand around chattering."

"Now, just a minute, just a minute." Martineau was holding up his hand.

The girls, on their way to their machines, stopped and looked at him.

"There will be no work tonight," he said. "Tomorrow we start on the Battle of Pointe Fortune, and I don't want everyone exhausted before we start."

"But these pants! We can't let them go!" Madame Tousignant was almost screaming.

"Yes we can," said Martineau.

"And let the Founding Fathers—" But Martineau cut her off.

"There is a simple solution," said Martineau. "Every pair of pants will have a little note pinned to it, addressed to the actor. It will warn him that for the sake of historical accuracy, the entry to the zipper is from the left rather than the right. This may make it a bit awkward for them to relieve themselves, but that is the way pants used to be, in the old days. If the actors are warned they will not panic."

"But that's not true," said Madame Tousignant. "The entry was *never* from the left."

"I know," said Martineau, "but actors are totally ignorant of such things. And now, girls, you may all go home."

There was a burst of applause from the seamstresses and Madame Tousignant marched away in a rage. Martineau, beaming with self-approval, put his hand on Lisette's arm.

"And now, my dear, he said, "I told you you weren't fired, but that doesn't mean you will continue in the sewing-room."

"Oh?" said Lisette, puzzled.

"Your true talents may lie elsewhere. You may require re-training. Have you ever thought of being a designer?"

"A *designer*! Oh, that would be marvellous."

"I would like to discuss it with you."

"Oh, sir, that would be so – so *good*. A designer!" Lisette's eyes, so recently washed by tears, were now glistening with excitement.

"Why don't we discuss it now?" said Martineau. "Can you come to my office?"

"Oh, yes, thank you!" And Lisette and Martineau walked off together toward his luxurious office, with its glove-leather di-van and its cabinet full of rare, smuggled liqueurs.

"Well," said Marie-Claire, "by tonight Lisette will know everything there is to know about the entry to the zipper."

Mona and Cecile laughed. And by tonight, Mona thought, *I* will know a lot more about *Paul*. She was surprised by the lasciviousness of her thought.

8

Some talk of Alexander,
    And some of Hercules;
Of Hector and Lysander,
    And such great names as these!

But of all the world's great heroes,
    There's none that can compare,
With a rah, and a rah, and a rah-rah-rah,
    To the British Grenadier!

All afternoon the song had been ringing in Paul's ears, for tonight he was to become an Anglo soldier – a fighter in the grand tradition of the British Grenadiers.

Tonight would be the turning point of his life; from this night onward he would be fighting for a noble cause, not just looking out for his own interests. "Arise ye Anglos!" he would be saying. "Like all other nations of the earth, great and small, we too can walk with our heads held high, in our own country!" That would be his message, punctuated by bombs.

It was an exhilarating thought, marred only by the fact that he couldn't tell Mona about it. But after he had belonged to the organization for a while he would ask for permission to bring her in on the secret. Surely that was not an unreasonable thing to ask. Who could be more trustworthy than Mona?

Paul flushed the toilet and left the bathroom. Outside, at the door, Colin Armitage was waiting for him. Armitage's face was even more haggard than usual, as though the ravages of his constipation had reached some new extremity.

"Would you do me a favour?" Armitage asked, nervously.

"Sure," said Paul. "If I can."

"I've drawn up this petition," said Armitage, producing a long sheet of paper. "It asks Mrs. MacVicar to extend the bathroom occupancy period from four minutes to eight minutes. I don't see how she can refuse, if everybody in the house signs." With a pleading look in his eye, he handed the petition to Paul, who read it.

"Believe me," said Armitage, "this will be good for all of us, not just me. A lot of the tension around this house would disappear if people could only sit back and relax in there."

"All right, I'll support you on this," said Paul. He took the pen that Armitage was thrusting at him and signed with a flourish. He noticed that so far only he and Armitage had signed.

"Thanks a million," said Armitage, grabbing the petition and striding down the hall toward Lionel Greenspoon's room.

As Paul went down the hall in the other direction, to his own room, he felt a twinge of regret at having signed the document. It wasn't the content, it was the style that bothered him: the grovelling language in which Armitage pleaded with Her Majesty Mrs. MacVicar for a very small scrap of mercy. It was typical of the Anglos of Montreal – broken and forever abject, thankful for every crumb from their masters' tables.

Well, all that would have to change. The population would have to be mobilized. Acts would have to be bold, statements forceful. The Armitage Petition, for instance, should have been written in thick, black strokes that said: "Mankind and Womankind Have a Right to Human Dignity in the Bathroom! The Anglo Liberation Army Will Fight the Four-Minute Rule and All Other Injustices! Down with the Enemy! Long Live Angloland (or New Canada)!"

Entering his room, Paul glanced at his watch. There was still half an hour to go before the supper bell. Then, right after supper, he would be meeting Chucky Dwyer up on Wellington

Street. Last night, in the park, Paul had told Mona that he wouldn't be able to see her tonight, that he would be off to play chess with Chucky. But actually he would be keeping a date with destiny.

As he thought about all this, Paul got down on his knees and reached under the bed. He pulled out a large, dusty cardboard box that was full of books. He opened one of them – a very old book, much fingered and grubby. It bore the title, *By Sheer Pluck: A Tale of the Ashanti War*, and it was by G.A. Henty. It told a thrilling story about the heroism and sacrifices of Queen Victoria's soldiers, as they struggled to bring law and order to the jungles of West Africa.

On the flyleaf of the book, a schoolboy had written his name in the careful penmanship of long ago: *James A. Pritchard, Montreal, Oct. 3, 1903.* He was Paul's great-grandfather.

James Pritchard's name was on the flyleaves of all the other G.A. Henty books that Paul kept in the box under his bed. They bore magical titles:

With Clive in India: The Beginnings of an Empire
On the Irrawaddy: A Tale of the First Burmese War
With Moore at Corunna: A Tale of the Peninsular War
The Tiger of Mysore: The War with Tipoo Saib
The Dash for Khartoum: A Tale of the Nile Expedition

These books took boys of an earlier era on a rousing march through the eighteenth and nineteenth centuries, as the British soldier gladly spilled his blood in strange and savage lands, to plant the Union Jack over a quarter of the world's surface, to present the Queen with necklaces of islands, to establish dominion over palm and pine. George Alfred Henty chronicled it all, for British boys wherever they might be, in Birmingham or Auckland or Capetown or Montreal.

By 1906, Paul's great-grandfather had read them all, and eight years later he was ready for his own war – the First World War – as a young lieutenant in the Royal Montreal Regiment. Paul often thought of James Pritchard, wearing the snappy breeches and the Sam Browne belt, boarding the troopship for

France; surely he must have heard G.A. Henty's trumpets and drums as the old *S.S. Andania* steamed down the St. Lawrence and out into the Atlantic. And he must have heard them again, on that cold morning of Easter Monday, in 1917, when he led his men into the German machine-guns, and died, at Vimy Ridge.

James's son, Frank Pritchard, had inherited the Henty books, and many years later he passed them on to his grandson, Paul. At the age of twelve, Paul started devouring them – probably the only boy in the whole Republic of Quebec ever to read fifteen obscure books by G.A. Henty.

Paul and his grandfather spent many happy hours discussing the world of these books – the insane bravery of the 21st Lancers at Omdurman, the difference in rank between a havildar and a risaldar-major, how you protected your flank in the Khyber Pass, and who were your most treacherous enemies – the Ashantis, the Boers, the Dervishes, the Pathans, the Afridis, or the Zakka-Khels.

"It's a damn shame Henty never lived to write about Vimy Ridge," Grandfather Pritchard would say. "That was the battle that created the Canadian nation. You should always remember that, Paul. Even though there's no more Canada, you're still a Canadian. You have that blood in you – the blood we shed on the battlefields of France. We Anglos went over there twice, in two wars, to bail them out. We died by the tens of thousands, but what thanks did we ever get from them?"

Grandfather Pritchard made little distinction between the French of France and the French of Quebec, and for him Separation was the ultimate ingratitude. "We should have gone to war with them, right after that referendum," he said. "We should have thrashed them the way we did at Crécy and Agincourt and Trafalgar and Waterloo."

Paul knew that his grandfather, if he were still alive, would applaud his decision to join the Anglo Liberation Army. "It's about time we stood up to them," the old man would say. "Remember, Paul, 'Britons never shall be slaves.'"

Paul put *By Sheer Pluck* back with the other books and dug

deeper into the cardboard box. He found what he was looking for – a small leather case. Inside the case, resting on a tiny bed of red velvet, was the Military Cross, the medal they awarded to his great-grandfather – posthumously – for his heroism at Vimy Ridge.

It was a beautiful medal, a silver cross suspended from a silver bar by a purple-and-white ribbon. There was a crown at the end of each arm of the cross and in the centre were the intertwined letters G.R.I. – the King's cipher.

Paul took the medal from its case and put it into his pocket. Now that it was his turn to go to war, this old Military Cross would be a talisman to give him courage and bring him luck.

He closed the cardboard box and slid it back under the bed. Then he left the room and went down the hall to Mona's room. He knocked on the door, but there was no answer. She had not come home from work yet. He went into the parlour, to wait for her and for the supper bell.

In the parlour, the television was on and the boarders were watching a documentary about the work of the *Bureau pour la rectification des monuments historiques*. As Paul sat down on the chesterfield, he watched technicians of the *Bureau* working on the bronze statue of Robert Burns, in Place Lévesque. The statue, which looked across at the former Windsor Hotel, had been erected long ago by the local admirers of the poet.

"This Robert Burns," the television commentator was saying, "symbolizes the greedy Anglo capitalists who exploited our people in Montreal for two hundred years. Today, accounts are being settled." The film now showed men with acetylene torches decapitating Robert Burns. As soon as the head came off, a new bronze head was welded on, that of Octave Boileau, a *Patriote* hero of the Rebellion of 1837. The plaque at the base of the statue was also replaced.

"Another monument rectified, another triumph for the *Bureau*," said the television narrator. "Today, the price of bronze is prohibitive. Thus this new technique of seamless neck-welding, perfected in the workshops of the *Bureau*, will be hailed throughout the world as a major breakthrough in the art of monumental sculpture."

"Disgusting," said Bud Sorenson, who was watching the television with the other boarders. "They're rewriting history, that's what they're doing."

"They're not rewriting history," said Lionel Greenspoon, "they're simply telling *their* history rather than someone else's." Greenspoon always spoke well of the French and this made him widely disliked among the other boarders.

"They keep talking about how they used to be an oppressed people," Sorenson said. "That really makes me laugh."

"The fact remains that before Separation they were not masters in their own house," said Greenspoon.

"Not masters? Don't make me laugh. When Quebec was a province, every member of the cabinet was French, every civil servant was French. And in Ottawa the Prime Minister of the whole country was French and half of *his* cabinet were French."

"It was O.K. for the big guys," said Greenspoon, "but the little guys always had to speak English to get a job."

"I'll tell you what, Greenspoon," said Sorenson, "I'm offering you a prize of ten piastres if you can tell me when, in the whole history of mankind, there was an oppressed people that were more *lightly* oppressed than the French Canadians. That's their real claim to fame – the most lightly oppressed people in history."

"If they were oppressed at all, it was wrong," said Greenspoon. "Can't you see that? It's a matter of dignity, not how deep are the wounds."

Just then Mona appeared in the doorway of the parlour. She beckoned to Paul and he went out into the hall to talk to her.

"Darling," she said, "something wonderful has happened."

"Oh?"

"Cathy's going out tonight. We can have the room to ourselves. And of course this is the night Mrs. MacVicar goes to her meeting."

She smiled at him, almost shyly, and he tried hard to make his own face look lovingly happy. But what he was feeling was shock, confusion, and dismay. This was the worst luck ever. How could he tell her that he could not go to bed with her tonight? That they could not do what they had been desperate to do for weeks.

"You'll have to cancel that chess game with Chucky," she said.

"Yes, I'll have to do that."

"Should you phone him now?"

"Uh, well, I think he probably isn't home yet. I'll, uh, phone him after supper."

The supper bell rang and they went into the dining-room.

"European Meatballs tonight," said Mrs. MacVicar, her ladle poised over her tureen. The boarders exchanged glances. This had never been on the menu before.

"You're not serving us horsemeat on Thursdays too, are you?" asked Doreen Brewster.

"Come, come, Miss Brewster," said Mrs. MacVicar. "You know very well that it's only on Mondays that I serve my economy meal." Mrs. MacVicar could never bring herself to utter the word "horsemeat."

Doreen seemed reluctant to start eating. She poked her fork suspiciously at the four ominous meatballs that sat in a puddle of gravy on her plate.

"If this isn't the old grey mare," she asked, "just what is it?"

"I'm afraid the recipe is secret," said Mrs. MacVicar. "But I assure you it's one of the better meats."

Paul too was having trouble eating. The conflict inside him was agonizing. Under the table he was holding Mona's hand; it was soft and sweet and it held the promise of incredible caresses, up there in bed. But that bed was out of the question, wasn't it? He had to be elsewhere tonight – in a cellar or in a remote shed, where men were making bombs and preparing to liberate their people. If he didn't show up tonight they would surely decide that he was not serious, and they would never ask him again.

"European Meatballs," Mr. Brophy was saying. "It's strange, Mrs. MacVicar, but I travelled extensively in Europe, during the Good Years, and I was never offered meatballs."

"Perhaps you didn't eat in the best places," said Mrs. MacVicar.

"In London I ate at the Savoy," said Mr. Brophy, "and in Zurich at the Baur au Lac. But there was never anything like this on the menu."

Paul managed to eat one of the meatballs, as well as the wedge of rubbery cabbage that went with it. But he was starting to feel sick with indecision. If he could only tell Mona where he had to go tonight. But he couldn't betray the A.L.A. What would she think? Would she be very angry? Would she break off their relationship because of this rejection?

He looked at her, sitting at his side, and their eyes met. He saw a promise in them, a promise of unimaginable bliss, and he suddenly realized how childish the A.L.A. was, and all it stood for. They were Boy Scouts, playing a preposterous game they could never win. But a profound and mature relationship with a woman, however, that was what life was all about.

"By the way," Colin Armitage was saying to Doreen, "would you mind having a look at this?" He handed her his petition and the ballpoint pen.

"If that's another petition about the food I serve, you're wasting your time," said Mrs. MacVicar.

"No, no," Armitage said, hastily, "it has nothing to do with the food."

"If you knew the price of groceries these days, Mr. Armitage," said Mrs. MacVicar, "you would know that I do very well with the small amount I can afford to spend. Of course if the government allowed me to raise the rent, things would be different."

"Heavens, Mrs. MacVicar, I think your cooking is excellent," Armitage said. "Tonight's meal is splendid. These, uh, meatballs have a very, uh, European flavour."

"Why, thank you, Mr. Armitage," said Mrs. MacVicar, beaming.

Spiro Costakis and Bud Sorenson exchanged a look of disgust. Was there nothing Armitage would not stoop to, to get his extra four minutes on the toilet?

"So you think these meatballs are delicious, do you?" said Doreen.

"Why, uh, yes," said Armitage, nervously.

"In that case, I'm afraid I can't sign your petition," said Doreen. "Unless we all put our foot down, we'll soon be eating horsemeat seven days a week."

She handed the petition and the ballpoint pen back to Armitage.

"I won't be able to sign that either," said Costakis.

"You'll have to count me out too," said Bud Sorenson.

Armitage, looking as though he was about to weep, got up suddenly and left the dining-room.

Dessert was a mealy kind of apple sauce, with bits of apple skin in it that clung to the roof of the mouth. Neither Paul nor Mona ate much of it.

"I guess you'd better phone Chucky," Mona said, "to cancel that chess game."

"Yes," said Paul, "I'd better do that." He had by now pretty well decided that his destiny lay with Mona and not with these Boy Scout guerrillas and their silly bombs.

As he got up from the table, Paul realized that the prospect of what he and Mona would soon be doing had caused him to sprout a stubborn erection. Would all the boarders notice it? He quickly put his hand into his pocket so they would think that the bulge in his pants was caused by the hand and not by his lust. As for Mona, she would think he was looking for a twenty-centime piece for the pay telephone down the hall.

"I'll wait for you in the room," she whispered in his ear.

"O.K. I'll just make the call and I'll be up," said Paul.

"Hurry," she said and, blowing him a kiss, she went up the stairs.

He went down the hall, walking stiffly with his hand in his pocket. But the hand had found something in the pocket and was fingering it. It was his talisman, for courage and luck, his great-grandfather's medal – the Military Cross. He took the medal out of his pocket and looked at it. In it he saw Lieutenant James Pritchard, of the Royal Montreal Regiment, in the mud of the trenches on that April morning of 1917. It was just before dawn. A quick swig of rum and then over the top – into the German guns.

Paul put a twenty-centime piece into the phone and started to dial. But then he stopped, for the ghost of his great-grandfather was speaking to him.

"Aren't you ashamed?" Lieutenant Pritchard asked. "Don't you know what your duty is?"

Paul dialled two more of the seven digits and then stopped again.

"That's the Anglos of today," the lieutenant said, bitterly. "They'll never make the smallest sacrifice. They deserve everything they get."

Abruptly, Paul put the receiver back on the hook. The twenty-centime piece tinkled inside the phone and tumbled down into the refund cup. Paul retrieved it, put it back in his pocket, and walked slowly up the stairs. He knocked on Mona's door, faintly and reluctantly. A moment later she opened it.

She had changed into a dressing gown, a thin, silky gown covered with small blue flowers. It hung very loosely and he could see a great deal of her ample breasts. She was, he guessed, completely naked under the dressing gown.

"Come in," she said, very softly.

"Mona, I don't know how to say this, but I . . . uh . . . I can't join you tonight."

"What?"

"It's . . . uh . . . not just a chess game with Chucky, it's a whole

94

tournament. If I drop out I ... uh ... spoil it for everybody."

She looked at him in silence. He wondered just what she was thinking; she knew, of course, that he was lying.

"I ... uh ... I'm really sorry," he mumbled. "I hope you'll understand."

"Am I dreaming this?" she said. "Are you really telling me that you'd rather play chess?"

"It's not what I'd rather do," he said miserably. "It's what I *have* to do. Please understand."

She stared at him, her eyes wide. Then, suddenly, she turned her back on him. He couldn't be sure, but he thought she might be starting to cry. He had expected anger, even fury, but not this. This was much worse. He wanted desperately to go to her and put his arms around her, to comfort her. But he knew that if he touched her he would be finished.

"Please ... uh ... trust me," he said. "Some day I'll explain."

"Get out," she said, in a flat voice. "Just get out."

There were tears starting in his own eyes as he closed the door and went down the stairs. Outside, on Rue Antonio Barrette, it was starting to drizzle. He wondered whether he should go back for his raincoat. But he couldn't be bothered. Moving slowly, as though in a trance, he unchained his bicycle, mounted it, and pedalled away in the darkness and the rain – to meet Chucky Dwyer and become a terrorist.

9

Paul arrived five minutes early at the Centre de Bicyclette Jacques Fortier, where they had agreed to meet. As instructed by Chucky, he joined the people who were wandering around, looking at the bicycles for sale.

Jacques Fortier was once a prosperous dealer in Dodge and Chrysler automobiles, but after Separation he had slowly phased out cars and phased in bicycles. Now, in the evenings, his showroom was a popular haunt for young Anglos. If you wanted to escape the suffocation of your boarding house, and didn't have the price of a beer, Fortier's was the place to go. It was a large, well-lit, and reasonably cheerful establishment, and the management didn't object to loitering.

The bicycles on display were stodgy, utilitarian imports from East Germany, or rakish but rickety machines from Viet Nam. The only Quebec-made model was the *Je Me Souvienscycle*, hand carved out of spruce and birch by the craftsmen of Baie St. Paul. This vehicle was heavily subsidized by the government as an example of post-industrial technology, but it was a poor seller, being prone to warping and splintering.

In the department that sold new bicycles, all the buyers were French. Anglos shopped in the second-hand section, where they browsed through rows of battered trade-ins. Paul walked quickly through both sections without seeing Chucky, so he went through to the repair shop, behind the showroom.

There were thirty-five mechanics here, tinkering away with aged, exhausted machines. As usual, there were many Anglo youths on hand, attracted by the Anglo girls waiting to have their bicycles repaired. Many a romance had started in this shop, often with a discussion about faulty brake calipers. But Chucky was not here either, so Paul went on to the glamorous department where pre-Separation bicycles were bought, sold, and exchanged.

In Quebec, vintage bicycle buffs considered themselves an aristocracy. They went without meals and without new clothes so they could keep their ancient machines in tip-top shape, and occasionally add exotic components. Nothing was more important to these fanatics than acquiring a Cinelli aluminum-alloy handlebar or a pair of Campagnolo Superlegerri pedals.

Paul joined a small crowd ogling a 1978 machine that had just been put on display – a gorgeous Raleigh Sprite with a trigger-control Sturmey Archer three-speed hub gear. It was in mint condition, a gleaming greyhound of a bicycle in black, green, and silver – a classic that no Anglo could ever hope to afford.

"In the old days, I used to buy bikes like that for my sons," somebody was saying, "and I never even looked at the price tag." It was Mr. Brophy, out for a walk with Doreen Brewster and Spiro Costakis.

"What did you ride yourself?" said Doreen.

"A Cadillac Seville," said Mr. Brophy, his face suddenly sad.

"Did Cadillac make bicycles, too?" said Costakis. "Or was it an automobile you had?"

"It was an automobile," Mr. Brophy said with a sigh. "It ran on gasoline."

Paul felt a tap on his shoulder and looked around. Chucky had arrived and together they strolled out of Fortier's. On the street they unchained their bicycles and pedalled away, toward Verdun.

"I thought I told you to wear dark clothes," Chucky said.

"Sorry," Paul said, "I forgot."

"You're going to have to use your head, Paul," Chucky said. "We're not playing games."

"It won't happen again. I promise."

Paul was wearing light-grey slacks and a beige windbreaker. He was much more visible in the dark than Chucky, whose slacks and raincoat were navy blue. Paul had meant to change after supper, but the dreadful scene with Mona had driven every other thought from his head.

They left Wellington Street and went up Rielle, a dingy residential street with a good deal of garbage in the gutters. It was starting to rain again, and again Paul realized that he had forgotten his raincoat. But there might be some virtue in this since his clothes would look darker as soon as they got wet.

They pedalled on, leaving Rielle Avenue and going down a back lane. Halfway down the lane they dismounted and chained their bicycles to a telephone pole. Then Chucky reached into his pocket and took out a pair of strange-looking goggles, of the sort aviators used to wear long ago, in the days of open cockpits. But the glass in the goggles was opaque.

"You're going to have to wear these," Chucky said, "to blindfold yourself."

"Oh? Why?"

"We don't want you to know where the meeting place is. Not until you're accepted into the organization."

"You mean they may not want me?"

"That's right. They have to look you over first."

Paul put on the goggles and found that he could see absolutely nothing, either straight ahead or to the side.

"I'm going to hold you by the elbow," Chucky said, "and you're going to hold this little white cane in your right hand. Whoever sees us on the street will see a blind man and his friend out for a walk."

They walked for what seemed to Paul to be a very long time, making frequent turns in and out of streets and lanes.

"O.K.," Chucky finally said. "Here we are."

He knocked three times at a wooden door and after a moment there was a single knock in reply. "Voltaire," Chucky said. This, presumably, was the password. Paul heard a bolt being drawn and the door open. Chucky guided him up two steps, into a room with what felt like a linoleum-covered floor. The door closed behind them. They crossed the room – was it a kitchen? – and went down a narrow flight of stairs into a basement, where Paul felt a cement floor underfoot.

"All right," said a man's voice, "get his clothes off, fast!"

Paul felt what seemed like a dozen hands grabbing hold of him, tearing off his windbreaker, unbuttoning his shirt, pulling off his shoes and socks.

"Hey, wait a minute!" he said. "I don't mind being wet. You don't have to do this."

"Shut up and stand still!"

"Look, I never catch cold. My clothes can dry *on* me."

"Will you stand still or do we have to hit you?"

Somebody pulled down Paul's zipper and he felt his pants falling to the floor. Then somebody pulled down his underwear. He was now naked.

"Let's see that flashlight," said a new voice, and Paul felt a pair of hands pulling apart the cheeks of his behind.

"Hey, what *is* this?" Paul cried out.

"Shut up!" said a voice. Paul winced as he felt something – was it the eraser at the end of a pencil? – probing his anus. Then, to his horror, someone pushed his testicles to one side and lifted up his penis.

"Hey!" Paul cried. "Chucky, are you here?"

"Sorry, Paul, but this has to be done," said Chucky. "They're looking for any miniature radio transmitters or homing devices, in case you're working for the police."

The fingers now probed Paul's armpits. Then they forced his mouth open and a pencil – he hoped it was a *different* pencil – poked into his cheeks and under his tongue.

"O.K.," said a voice. "He's clean."

"You can get dressed now," said another voice.

"Can I take these goggles off?" Paul said.

"No," said the first voice. "And don't speak unless you're spoken to."

Getting dressed while blindfolded, with clothes that were

soaking wet, proved to be quite difficult, and it took him a long time. When he finished, an authoritative voice addressed him.

"I'm the commander of this cell," the voice said. "I want to know if you're willing to take orders."

"Yes, sir, I am."

"Even if the orders sound stupid to you?"

"That doesn't matter, sir. I'll carry out any orders that are given to me." This was something Paul had learned from the G.A. Henty books. The British soldier was often asked to do dangerous things that didn't make any sense. But he always did as he was ordered.

"It's important for you to realize," the commander said, "that even though we're fighting for democracy, this *cell* isn't a democracy. It's a military unit, not a debating society. Everybody follows orders. Is that clear?"

"Perfectly clear, sir."

Paul heard a door open and somebody either come in or go out. There was some whispering. While he waited for the next question – or order – he found himself thinking of the British soldiers in the Siege of Mafeking and Captain Vernon's suicidal assault on the enemy blockhouse. Now *that* was what you'd call following orders...

"Do you hate the French?" the commander asked, abruptly.

"No, sir," said Paul. "I don't."

"Are you sure of that?"

"Yes, sir."

Paul felt a hard slap across his face. The commander had hit him with what must have been the back of his hand.

"Don't lie to me," said the commander. "You know you hate the French."

The shock of the slap knocked Paul's breath away and his heart thumped wildly.

"You must always tell me the truth," the commander said.

Paul felt an impulse to leap into the darkness and flail out at the man who had slapped him. But something made him restrain himself.

"Now tell me *why* you hate them," the commander said.

"But I *don't* hate them," Paul said.

There was a long silence and Paul wondered whether he had disqualified himself. Perhaps you *had* to hate the French if you wanted to join the A.L.A. But actually Paul liked them very much – or at least the ones with whom he came into contact. They were, he felt, decent, intelligent, warm-hearted, civilized people. They had qualities that many Anglos lacked. But they had been betrayed by their leaders, who had given them this rotten government. And they had been betrayed by their intellectuals, who had been so busy waving Quebec's flag that they had forgotten to defend its freedoms.

Paul had to admit that he personally had never met a French intellectual – they were far removed from his workaday orbit – but he remembered Mr. Brophy telling him what a dubious lot they were, back in the days when Quebec was still part of Canada. Their parochialism was legendary. They were, for instance, totally ignorant about every aspect of the culture of English Canada, but that didn't prevent them from insisting that this culture didn't even exist. Also, their idea of humour was to make tasteless jokes about the Queen.

"If you don't hate the French, how are you going to fight them?" the commander asked.

"I don't want to fight the French, I want to fight the government," Paul said. "Besides, you don't have to hate to fight. Take Baden-Powell at Mafeking. He didn't hate the enemy. In fact, he wrote very polite letters to General Cronje, who was besieging him. And General Cronje answered him. They wrote to each other almost every day, while the siege went on. But that didn't prevent Baden-Powell from *shooting* at Cronje, did it?"

"What the hell is he talking about?" came a voice from the darkness.

"It's the Boer War, I think," said Chucky. "Paul is quite an expert on things like that." Chucky sounded embarrassed.

"The Siege of Mafeking," Paul said. "It began on October

101

14, 1899, and it lasted for 217 days."

This remark seemed to provoke a good deal of whispering among the cell members, and Paul wondered whether he had gone on too much about Mafeking. People who weren't students of British history mightn't be all that interested. He wondered whether he ought to point out that the siege had made Baden-Powell the greatest hero since Wellington, but now the commander was addressing him again.

"Tell us why you want to join the Anglo Liberation Army," the commander said.

Chucky had warned Paul that this question would probably come up, and Paul had his answer ready, well-rehearsed.

"I think we Anglos have a historic right to self-determination," he said. "Our language and our culture are in danger of disappearing. We need our own country, just as any other nation does. If Quebec was able to separate from Canada, we should be able to separate from Quebec."

Having said this, Paul waited uneasily, wondering what other questions they might have for him. Then somebody's hand came up to his face and took off his goggles. He saw that he was in the middle of a dimly-lit basement with a furnace in it. Facing him was a dark, burly man in his fifties.

"Congratulations," the man said, shaking Paul's hand. "You're now a member of the General Wolfe Cell of the Anglo Liberation Army. My name is Guido. I'm your commander."

"I'm proud to be with you," said Paul. It was a line he had been rehearsing in his mind.

"Congratulations," said Chucky.

"Let me introduce some of our members," Guido said. Paul shook hands with them as they were introduced: Robert, a scholarly-looking youth of nineteen or twenty; Margaret, a thin, tough-looking woman in her early thirties; Harry, a nervous man of about thirty-five; Stuart, who looked like a boxer; and Janet, a matronly woman, possibly a housewife.

"We go by first names here," Guido said. "We don't learn each other's surname unless we have to. Now let's go inside."

102

Chucky opened a door and they went into another part of the basement, a large room finished with plywood panelling, with a bar at the end. In pre-Separation days, this might have been called a "rumpus room," but now it probably housed a whole Anglo family. There was a double bed as well as two cots and several chairs. The cell members sat down on the chairs and the edges of the cots.

"There's one thing I should explain, Paul," Guido said. "When I accused you of lying, I didn't really think you were lying. I'm sure you don't hate the French. But I wanted an opportunity to slap your face. I wanted to see how you would react, how you would respond to discipline."

"Our members should be highly motivated, but they shouldn't lose their tempers too easily," said the woman called Margaret. "Self-control is essential. You passed that test very well."

"You may be surprised to see that there are only seven of us here," Guido said. "There are three more members who you will meet in due time. No cell has more than twelve members. There are, of course, other cells, but there is no need for most of us to know how many."

Guido explained to Paul that meetings were held irregularly, and at different places, to throw the police off the track. He outlined the complex method by which members were kept informed as to when and where they should meet. Then he moved on to the main business of the evening – a discussion of ways and means to disrupt the forthcoming celebrations that would mark the twentieth anniversary of the Separation of Quebec.

"In the words of Winston Churchill, this will be our finest hour," Guido said. "We're going to make it an anniversary that Quebec will never forget."

* * *

After the meeting, Paul and Chucky pedalled homeward.

"That Guido's quite a guy, isn't he?" Paul said.

103

"He's a very tough character," Chucky said. "And a born leader."

"An Italian?"

"Yes. Don't forget, the Italians in Montreal have been fighting the French since before Separation, when the French first started forcing Italian kids to go to French schools."

"Makes you wonder, doesn't it? How can the French be so proud of their language when they have to *force* people to speak it? You'd think they'd be ashamed."

"Guido used to be a wealthy man," Chucky said. "He and his father owned a big restaurant up on Jean Talon Street. But he was always in trouble with the language laws, with their menu. First they forced him to change veal scallopine to *escalope de veau*; then macaroni had to become *tuyaux miniatures de pâtes alimentaires*. Then they had to find French words for spaghetti, minestrone, lasagna, ravioli and cassata. Zuppa inglese had to become *soupe à la culture minoritaire*. But Guido said the food just didn't taste the same without the Italian name.

"Well, he fought them dish by dish, all the way down the menu. But when they came to fettucine Alfredo, the *Office pour la défense de la langue de la patrie* couldn't agree among themselves on a French word for fettucine. They spent a small fortune consulting linguistic purity experts from France, Switzerland, Belgium, everywhere – but they couldn't reach an agreement, so they told Guido to take fettucine Alfredo off his menu completely, until they decided.

"Guido was very angry by then, and he refused. So they closed the restaurant down, for good. But Guido dreams of reopening some day, when freedom is restored. As he says, 'When pasta is once again pasta.'"

* * *

The next day Guido and Chucky met in Guido's house to discuss strategy.

"I just hope he's going to work out all right," Guido said.

"Don't worry," said Chucky, "Paul is a very solid citizen, very reliable."

"The way he talks about the Boer War is kind of weird, isn't it?"

"That's harmless, Guido. It's just his hobby. He reads all kinds of old books."

"And you're sure his girlfriend is really beautiful?" Guido asked.

"Yes, she's a knockout," said Chucky.

"I still wonder," Guido said, "whether we shouldn't have figured out a way to approach the girl ourselves, without going through Paul."

"It wouldn't have been a good idea," Chucky said. "Like I told you, this Mona is only interested in escaping to the States. We could never recruit her except through Paul. He's the only person who could ever politicize her."

"Goddam it," Guido said. "Why does it have to be so hard to find a beautiful, sexy woman?"

"Listen, Guido," Chucky said. "Paul Pritchard is going to be a big asset to us, in his own right. He's got guts. He'll do a lot more for this cell than just bring in the girl."

"Why are our own sisters in this organization so—so goddam *homely*?"

"Because beauties don't join revolutions, that's why. They've got other fish to fry."

"But we absolutely *have* to have a gorgeous dame for Operation Thunderbolt."

"I notice you didn't tell the members about Thunderbolt last night."

"No, it's too risky. The fewer of us who know about it the better, until the time comes."

"Do you really think we can bring it off, Guido?"

"Why shouldn't we bring it off?"

"Well, it's so—so fantastic."

"If we get any breaks at all we'll succeed. And it'll be our biggest victory ever."

"It'll really bring independence a lot closer, won't it?"

"Yes, Chucky, it will. But I wish so much didn't depend on us recruiting a sexy woman. And a woman with a hell of a lot of courage."

"Don't worry, Guido. Mona is going to be just right for Thunderbolt."

10

Of all the projects celebrating the twentieth anniversary of Separation, none excited the imagination of the people of Montreal more than the dismantling of the old Cross on top of Mount Royal, in the centre of the city. The Cross, thirty metres high, had been erected in 1924. Since then its bright lights had beamed a message of hope through some of the darkest nights in the history of Quebec. But now, according to the *Bureau du symbolisme national*, the old Cross no longer reflected the principal aspirations of the nation. Its steel girders would be carefully stored, to be re-erected at some future date, as part of a projected Museum of the Colonial Era.

In the place where the Cross had stood, the *Bureau* was putting up a gigantic letter Q – for Quebec – fashioned out of aluminum. At precisely one minute after midnight on June 24, President Chartrand would press a button and illuminate the Q. A halo of dazzling light would crackle around its edges, light so bright that it would be visible seventy kilometres away, well across the border into the United States.

The moment the light went on, according to the *Bureau du symbolisme*, there would be exuberant cheers from the crowds in the streets below, especially when they noticed that the tail of the Q had been programmed to flick up and down, three times every two seconds. There would be much praise for the *Bureau* for having devised this ingenious way of proclaiming the virility of the young republic.

As they sat at their Sunday morning breakfast, Mrs. Mac-

Vicar's boarders listened to the latest news about the Q on Lionel Greenspoon's portable radio. "...*trois fois plus brillant que la Tour Eiffel*," the announcer was saying, "*la lumière du Q national ...*"

"Come on, Lionel, turn it off," Doreen Brewster said. "We've had enough."

"Just a minute," Greenspoon said. "I find this very interesting."

"...*certainement le plus grand Q du monde entier...*"

Mona glanced across the table at Paul, but when his eyes met hers she looked away. Two days had passed since his inexplicable behaviour of Thursday night. During that time Mona's emotions had fluctuated between hurt and anger. This morning anger predominated, and when Paul had attempted to sit down beside her at the breakfast table she had moved across to the other side.

"That Q would be funny if it wasn't tragic," Bud Sorenson said. "Why don't they spend the money on building a factory, something that will *produce* something?"

"These people are rediscovering their pride," Lionel Greenspoon said. "Like all other nations they need their symbols. Especially after two centuries of exploitation."

"Balls," said Sorenson. "What they need to do is create some kind of an economy, not just sell electricity to Russia."

Mona glanced at Paul again and noted with satisfaction that he seemed to be unhappy, poking aimlessly with his spoon at Mrs. MacVicar's watery porridge. During the past two days he had tried, on several occasions, to have a conversation with Mona, but in each case she had cut him short, with cold formality. He kept insisting that he had had to play in a chess tournament that night, and kept saying that she would understand "some day." But it was obvious that he was lying. He had probably been with another woman, but Mona was too proud to confront him with her suspicion.

"I'm surprised, Bud, that you want them to *create* wealth," Spiro Costakis was saying. "Anybody can *create* wealth. What takes real brains is knowing how to divide it up properly among what they call 'the collectivity.' That's a specialty in Quebec – *dividing* the wealth."

"Except there's nothing left to divide."

"You guys are really funny," Greenspoon said. "For you everything is materialism. These people are struggling to maintain their identity, surrounded by a hostile continent. Their very identity. That's a lot more important than another lousy factory in a plastic world."

"Well, they're doing pretty good in the struggle against materialism," Sorenson said. "Did you notice this year's graduating class at the University of Montreal? Two thousand sociologists, anthropologists, and criminologists – and three engineers."

"Yeah," said Costakis. "And two of those three engineers are working on that big Q on top of the mountain."

Mona finished her coffee and left the table. Paul followed her into the hall.

"I was wondering if you'd like to go for a walk," he said.

"No thanks," she said. "I'm busy."

"Then could we have a talk?"

"What about?"

"Well, uh, nothing in particular. Just a talk."

"I'm sorry, I have to be on my way."

She was pleased to note the distress in his face as she walked past him down the hallway and out the front door. They almost always went for a walk after breakfast on Sundays, but today Mona would visit her parents instead. She wanted to break the news to them that as soon as the snow came she would be leaving for the United States. By telling them now she would be giving them six months or so to get used to the idea.

She would be going alone, now that she was finished with Paul, but it occurred to her that perhaps her sister Naomi would want to come with her. Two people could cope so much better than one with the ordeal of snowbacking. And surely Naomi realized that she had no future in Quebec. But Naomi was so difficult, so sullenly idealistic, so critical of Mona for working at *l'Atelier*. Could she be persuaded to overcome her animosity, and form a partnership that would take them both to a better life, in the States? As she started off on her bicycle, Mona wondered just what words she should use to sell the idea to her sister.

Mona's parents and their younger daughter lived on Rue St. Dominique. It was in this area, in the narrow old streets just east of Boulevard St. Laurent, that most of Montreal's Jews had first settled, in their big immigrations from Eastern Europe at the end of the nineteenth century and the beginning of the twentieth.

As the Jews prospered after the First World War they left this area and moved westward to the streets around Avenue du Parc. After the Second World War there was yet another west-ward migration, this time to the Snowdon district. By the time Separation came, most of the city's Jews were living still farther west, in tidy suburbs like Côte St. Luc and Chomedy, where they built ranch-style bungalows and maisonettes in the style of the ante-bellum South.

But after the Nine Good Years, the Linguistic Purity Laws reduced the Jews, like all the other Anglos, to dire poverty. They could no longer afford the property taxes of Côte St. Luc, so they were forced to sell their houses to the French, for a fifth of their value. And, perhaps driven by some primordial instinct, they moved back to Boulevard St. Laurent and the shabby streets nearby. This was the old "Main Street" of song and story, the old ghetto where their great-grandparents, from Cracow and Bucharest and Odessa, had gained their first toe-hold on freedom, finally safe from the whips of the Cossacks. And now, as Mona's father put it, "We're back at square one."

Jack and Gloria Rosenstein lived in a small red-brick row house that was more than a hundred years old. The south side of the house seemed to be sinking into the ground at an almost perceptible rate; every time Gloria dropped a spool of thread it rolled down the slanting floor with a velocity that seemed

110

greater than the last time. This sometimes upset Gloria to the point of hysteria, but Jack was, as always, philosophical. "Don't let it get to you," he would say. "Just imagine we're on a ship, a luxurious cruise ship in the sunny West Indies." Jack kept saying this, although it only aggravated Gloria's distress. "I wish it *was* a ship," she would say. "I'd jump overboard."

Mona tethered her bicycle to a lamp post outside the sinking house and twisted the tinny old doorbell. After quite some time, her mother came to the door. But instead of greeting Mona, Gloria Rosenstein turned and shouted back into the house. "Surprise!" she called out. "The princess is honouring us with a visit."

"Not so loud, Mrs. R.," came a man's voice from upstairs. "It's Sunday and the wife is still asleep." It was Mr. Glickman, head of one of the two other families that shared the small house with the Rosensteins.

Mona closed the door and followed her mother down the long hallway. She noted with distaste that her mother was still wearing her hundred-year-old bathrobe, more torn and faded than ever, and her two-hundred-year-old slippers, which shuffled noisily on the orange-and-mauve linoleum of the hall. Her mother's hair was in curlers; at least she hadn't given up completely on her appearance.

"A delegation has arrived," Gloria announced, as they entered the living-room. "A delegation from the aristocracy of Point St. Charles."

"Hi," said Naomi. She examined Mona briefly and then went back to her sewing.

"Hi, Naomi," said Mona. "Hi, Papa."

But Jack Rosenstein didn't answer. He was sitting cross-legged on the floor, meditating. He held up the index finger of his right hand in what could be either an expression of Hindu wisdom or a request that Mona wait a moment, until he was free to speak.

"This week it's yoga," Gloria said. "That's the lotus position."

111

"What about the bio-feedback?" Mona said.

"That's finished, thank God. At least with this yoga he doesn't have to rent an expensive machine."

"Would you rather that I drank?" said Jack Rosenstein, getting to his feet. "Or ran around with women?"

"Just do me a favour and stop buying books," Gloria said. "You don't need a book to teach you how to stare into space."

"How are you, sweetheart?" said Jack, kissing Mona on the forehead. "You look great."

"I'm fine, Papa. How are you?"

"I'm reaching a state of equilibrium, if you know what I mean. I'd like to talk to you about it, but later."

"And to what do we owe the honour of this visit?" Gloria asked.

"Look, Ma, I just came to see you, that's all."

"In that case it must be Rosh Hashana. Or is it Passover, and I forgot?" Gloria had never forgiven her daughter for moving out of the family home, a year ago. But at that time Mona had felt that she could not endure even one more day in it – bearing the brunt of her mother's bitterness, sleeping with Naomi on the hide-a-bed in the so-called living-room, and listening to the endless wrangles with the Glickmans and the Weinbergs in the greasy kitchen that had to be shared by three families.

"Are you still working for the enemy?" Naomi asked, looking up from her sewing.

"As a matter of fact, I'm going to be leaving *l'Atelier*," Mona said. "It's not that I'm doing anything wrong by working there, it's just that I think there's a better future somewhere else."

"Where's that?" said Naomi. "Are you going to work for the secret police?"

"Come on, Naomi, don't be so hard on her," said Jack Rosenstein.

"I'm going to the States," Mona said. "To New York. As soon as winter comes."

"Isn't that wonderful," Gloria said. "You'll abandon your family to their fate."

"Give her a chance," Jack said. "Let's listen to her reasons."

"I think I could make something of myself down there," Mona said. "I could eventually earn good money. Then you could come down and join me. It would be a new life for us all."

"I can just see your father and me running through the snowstorm," Gloria said, "with the border patrol shooting at us."

"Why don't you come with me, Naomi?" Mona said. "You too could make something of yourself down there. How about it?"

"Isn't that beautiful?" Gloria said. "Tear your family in half, just like that."

"Let's hear them out, Gloria," Jack said. "Give them a chance. They have their whole life in front of them."

"You don't have to worry," Naomi said. "I'm not going."

"Do you want to spend the rest of your life washing out bottles and sorting out rags and junk?" said Mona.

"No, I don't," Naomi said. "But I'm going to do something about it. Not just for myself but for my people too. You might as well know, Ma, that I'm going to join the Anglo Liberation Army."

"Well, we're certainly getting a lot of news today," Jack said.

"That's all I need," Gloria said. "One daughter is shot by the border patrol and the other one is in jail for throwing bombs. Or maybe even in front of the firing squad." Gloria was now pacing up and down the living-room, her decrepit slippers slapping fretfully against the slanting floor.

"Snowbacks are cop-outs," Naomi said. "Anyone with guts stays and fights."

"You're only seventeen," Gloria said. "You're too young for any kind of army."

"Violence is not necessarily the answer," Jack said. "Mohandas K. Gandhi speaks of the efficacy of passive resistance. I could get you a book on the subject."

"We don't need any more books," Gloria said. "What we need is a new second-hand sofa. One where the springs aren't popping out."

"I have a library of eleven books and she thinks I'm over-stocked," Jack said. "And only four of those books are in English. The rest I have trouble understanding. Reading philosophy in French is not easy."

"How are you going to go about joining this Liberation Army?" Mona said to Naomi. "Do you know anybody in it?"

"No, I don't," said Naomi. "But I'll find out."

"She'll put an ad in the paper to inquire," Gloria said. "She'll include our name and address."

Jack Rosenstein got to his feet and pulled on his sweater. "I'm going out on my rounds," he said. "Maybe you'd like to come with me, Mona."

"Yes, I would," Mona said. It was years since she had been out with her father, and this would be a good chance to talk to him without bitter interventions from her mother and Naomi.

In the yard behind the house Jack Rosenstein hitched his old white horse, Alphonse, to his wagon. Mona climbed up beside him and they set off down the lane.

"Is Alphonse all right?" Mona said. "He doesn't look too good."

"It's old age," Jack said. "Another year, I figure, and then it's the glue factory. It'll break my heart."

"Will you be able to afford a new horse?"

"Who knows?"

They clattered down the lane, past dilapidated sheds and stables, past children playing with hoops, past women hanging out their washing on intricate networks of rope.

"*J'achète des bouteilles!*" Jack Rosenstein shouted, in a sing-song voice. "*J'achète du linge! J'achète des objets usagés!*"

In the new Quebec, Jews dominated the scrap and junk business, and they were prominent in other recycling trades, such as repairing shoes, mending clothing, retreading bicycle tires, and patching up holes in pots and pans. These were all one-man or family businesses; an entrepreneur who employed even one person who was not a member of his immediate family had to pass the Linguistic Purity Test, and this, of course, was impossible. In Jack Rosenstein's business, Gloria and Naomi were the sole employees. They washed the bottles he bought, for resale to breweries and pharmacies; they ground up the old bones, to be sold as fertilizer; and they sorted the rags, for export to Algeria, where they were made into fine paper.

"*Vas-y, Alphonse! Vas-y, mon beau!*" Jack cried, urging his weary old horse across Avenue du Parc.

"What would you think, Pa, if I were to go to the States?" Mona said.

"Are you really unhappy in your work?" Jack said.

"Yes, there's no future in it at all."

"You know, in yoga we are told that there is no future and no past. Everything around us is unreal. The only reality lies within ourselves. That is where we must find happiness – inside ourselves, through meditation. If you believe this, changing jobs or getting rich or moving away doesn't mean anything. All the answers are inside ourselves. I'm getting a lot of comfort out of that, Mona. Maybe it could help you, too. Maybe you should start meditating."

"I don't think it would help, Pa."

"There is no future and there is no past. For all I know there is no present either, but I'm not sure. I haven't read deeply enough. Your mother won't let me buy any more books."

"How does this yoga differ from the power of positive thinking? Or psycho-cybernetics?" Mona said this without sarcasm; she was genuinely interested in knowing. She much preferred her father's hopeful quest for enlightenment to her mother's unwavering pessimism.

"Those systems, I have concluded, are philosophically unsound," Jack said. "But I would really like to do some more reading on the subject. I hear a rumour, by the way, that they may allow the English libraries to re-open, on a limited basis. Do you hear anything about that?"

"That's a rumour that's always going around," Mona said. "I'll believe it when I see it."

After the Nine Good Years, and the Great Riots, the government had padlocked all English public libraries in Montreal and had closed down all English bookshops. This was necessary, President Chartrand explained, because a survey by government sociologists showed that there existed in the city more books in English than in French, and this constituted "residual cultural aggression," a hangover from the Colonial Era. There was no reason why books should escape the "rectification of cultural proportions" that had curtailed the "alien cacophony" of the city's English-language radio, television, and newspapers.

The padlocking was a temporary measure, the President said. It was part of the State of Emergency; the libraries would re-open as soon as Quebec's French culture was out of danger from the "destabilizing and re-colonializing plots of the purveyors of the minority media."

The Emergency was now in its eleventh year, but the authorities felt that the continuing lack of English books should pose no great hardship for anyone. Anglos who sought after knowledge, they said, should read *French* books; there was no branch of learning that had not been written about as well – and usually better – in French as in English. As for the English classics, such as Shakespeare and Dickens, most Quebec scholars were convinced that they had more artistic merit in French translation than in the original.

"If you escape to the States you'll have the luxury of books," Jack Rosenstein said.

"Yes," said Mona. "It'll be strange living in an all-anglophone world."

"I wish you wouldn't use those awful words 'anglophone' and 'francophone,'" Jack said. "I may be old-fashioned, but

116

those are French words that have no place in the English language. If we want our culture to survive we must at all costs protect the purity of the Anglo English that's spoken in Montreal. We can't let it get corrupted by French words, the way the French they speak in Quebec has been corrupted by English words."

"What would you say instead of 'anglophone?'" Mona asked.

"I'd say 'English-speaking,' what else?" said Jack. "Or 'English-speaking people.'"

Alphonse was now pulling the wagon up the lane behind Avenue de l'Epée. This was French territory, and it was here that most of Jack Rosenstein's clientele lived, in houses that were in only slightly better repair than those of the Anglos.

"*J'achète des bouteilles!*" Jack sang out. "*J'achète du linge!*"

Hearing his cry, a housewife came out through her back door and waved for him to stop.

"*Bonjour, Monsieur Jack!*" she called out.

"*Bonjour, Madame Poupart,*" Jack said.

Madame Poupart had only a few newspapers to sell, and some shiny bones that no longer had any shreds of meat or marrow to contribute to her soup pot. Jack weighed these items carefully on his scale and paid her for them. Then he flicked his reins and the wagon started off again down the lane.

"*J'achète des objets usagés!*" he cried. "*J'achète vos trésors!*"

"If I go to the States," Mona said, "do you think I would be abandoning you, the way Ma says?"

"I would hate to see you leave us, sweetheart, but you should go if you think it's best. You have your whole life in front of you."

"I wish Naomi would come with me."

"What about that young man of yours – Paul? Isn't he interested in going to the States?"

"I'm finished with Paul, Papa."

"Oh? I'm sorry to hear that. He sounded nice."

"Well, he's not nice."

"What happened?"

"I'd rather not talk about it, if you don't mind."

Mona had told her father about Paul, but not her mother, who would never have approved of him. Paul was not only non-Jewish, but he was a farmer, which would be a very lowly occupation in Gloria's eyes.

In the new Quebec, Jewish mothers could no longer aspire to their daughters' marrying doctors or lawyers, as there were no longer any Jewish doctors or lawyers, thanks to the Linguistic Purity Laws. But there were certain occupations that carried more status than others, and it was here that a mother's hopes could reside. Shoe repairmen, for instance, ranked high in Jewish society. Not only did they earn relatively good money, but they were endowing their ancient craft with a new dignity. They called themselves "footwear revitalizers," and if you brought a particularly dilapidated pair of shoes to your neighbourhood revitalizer, shoes that were possibly beyond redemption, he might ask if he could call in a colleague for a "consultation." This would cost you a few centimes more, but it was considered wise to get "another opinion." Footwear revitalizers used words like "gestalt" and "fixation" in their conversation and there was talk of their asking the authorities for permission to start a learned journal dealing with new developments in their science.

"I wanted to speak to you about Naomi," Jack was saying.

"Oh?" Mona said. "Is there anything wrong?"

"Do you think she's serious about joining the Anglo Liberation Army?"

"Has she talked about it before?"

"No, today is the first time she's mentioned it."

"I don't want to scare you, Papa, but with Naomi I think it's quite possible."

"I think so too. I'm worried about her, Mona. She's so young to be involved in something so dangerous."

They left the lane behind Avenue de l'Epée, crossed Rue St. Viateur and entered another lane. Business was brisker here, with several housewives coming out with their accumulations of bottles, rags, bones, tin cans, newspapers and household detritus of every description.

Jack Rosenstein deftly weighed each item on his rusty scale, did a lightning calculation in his head, and paid the vendor the exact amount. Some of the calculations were quite complex, and some housewives checked his figures with pencil and pad. But Jack was never wrong.

"I'm amazed you never make a mistake," Mona said.

"It's nothing amazing," Jack said. "After all, I'm a chartered accountant, am I not?"

He said it without bitterness or irony; and Mona, feeling a surge of pity and affection, leaned over and kissed him on the cheek. She so admired his quiet and uncomplaining ways, his adjustment to life, his "philosophy."

At the same time, she had to admit that she admired her sister Naomi for opposite qualities. Naomi was a grumbler and a noisy complainer, but she was always idealistic and uncompromising. Tomorrow Naomi would be helping her family by sorting out these wretched rags her father was now buying, and washing these sticky bottles. While Naomi was doing this, in the grimy shed behind her parents' house, Mona would be sitting in the airy sewing-room of *l'Atelier*, making costumes that would glorify the oppressors of her people and their deplorable Proclamation of Sovereignty.

Was Naomi going to become a freedom fighter, a member of the A.L.A.? Mona would not be in the least surprised. She and her sister were so very different. Mona's mother had summed up that difference, quite succinctly, on the day Mona moved out of the family home. "Naomi may not be as pretty as you are," Gloria said, "she may be overweight and she may not be as smart as you are. But there is one thing she has, Mona, that you never had. She is *not selfish*."

11

Paul's first mission for the A.L.A. was to help steal some dynamite, from which bombs could be made. Now, at midnight, he and Chucky were on their bicycles, moving through the wastelands at the extreme eastern end of the Island of Montreal. There were huge oil refineries here, mazes of tanks and pipes and catwalks that were once brightly lit at night, with great flames thrusting high into the air to burn off waste gases. But when the automobile disappeared from Quebec, the refineries closed down, and now the towering machinery was dark and silent, like an abandoned space station on a dead planet.

Paul and Chucky left the refineries behind them and headed down a desolate side road. Finally they reached their destination, a quarry that formed a huge crater in the ground. They got off their bicycles and sat at the edge of the crater, looking down into it. They sat in silence for twenty minutes and then Chucky spoke. "There's no watchman," he said. "Let's go."

They walked slowly down the gravel-covered road that led into the quarry. At the bottom there was a shed. It was unlocked and they went in. Chucky turned on his flashlight and they quickly examined the dust-covered shelves and bins. But except for a few old shovels, there was nothing in the shed.

"Goddam it!" Chucky said.

"Quiet!" Paul whispered. "Somebody's coming."

From the path outside the shed they heard footsteps crunching in the gravel. Chucky picked up a shovel and held it ready to bring down on the visitor's head, should he prove to be hostile. At the same time he handed the flashlight to Paul. "Point the light into his eyes when the door opens," he whispered.

The footsteps drew closer and finally the door opened. But then, as the flashlight found the intruder's face, Chucky put down his shovel. "For God's sake," he said, "it's Norman."

"Who's that?" said the man in the doorway.

"It's Chucky. Come on in."

"Chucky? Is that really you?"

"Yeah. I guess we're looking for the same thing you are."

"Who's this with you?"

"This is Paul. He's new. Paul, meet Norman. He's from another cell."

"Pleased to meet you," said Paul, and he and Norman shook hands.

"Find anything?" Norman asked.

"No, damn it," Chucky said.

"Christ!" Norman said. "Last night I went way out to that Pointe Claire quarry and there was nothing there either."

"I guess there are just no quarries that are working," Chucky said.

"It makes sense," Norman said. "There's no construction going on anywhere in Quebec, so there's no need for stone. No quarrying, no dynamite."

"No construction at all?" Chucky said. "I figured there's always some new country houses going up for cabinet ministers or army officers."

"Yeah, but most of that work is done in the summer."

"What the hell are we going to do for dynamite, Norman?"

"That's the sixty-four piastre question, isn't it? We've only got four sticks left in our whole cell."

"At least you've got four," Chucky said. "We've got bugger all."

"Shit!" Norman said. "It gets more discouraging every day, doesn't it?"

They left the shed and trudged up the gravel road. At the

top of the quarry Paul and Chucky mounted their bicycles and waved goodbye to Norman as they set off toward Montreal. Three cyclists would attract more attention from the police than two, so Norman would wait for them to disappear down the road before setting off himself.

"God, how I envy those old Separatist terrorists of the 1960s," Chucky said, as they pedalled through the darkness. "They really had it made, in the F.L.Q. Canada was prosperous so Quebec was prosperous and there was construction everywhere. In one night you could steal enough dynamite to blow up every mailbox in the city."

"Wouldn't it be nice if we could do it *without* dynamite?" said Paul. "Without violence."

"Naturally that's the way we'd *like* to do it," said Chucky. "And that's the way we *will* do it, if they give us our referendum. All we want is the same thing they had – a referendum on our own territory, which is the western half of Montreal and the Eastern Townships."

"They'll never give us a referendum," said Paul.

"Don't be too sure," said Chucky.

Again they cycled past the dark skeletons of the oil refineries. In the old days, you would have seen the glittering lights of Montreal from here, in the distance. But now, at night, the city was just a huge, inert mass of blackness; Quebec no longer had any electricity to spare for lighting up cities at night; every possible watt had to be piped across the North Pole to Russia, to earn the rubles that were the lifeblood of the young republic.

"By the way," Chucky said, "how's Mona these days?"

"I'm not too sure," Paul said.

"Is there something wrong?"

"She's not talking to me. At least not very much."

"What's the problem?"

"I think she thinks I'm seeing another woman. I can't tell her where I'm going on nights like this, and she just doesn't buy that chess tournament story."

"So she's mad as hell?"

"Yes, she's very, very cold. I'm going to ask Guido if I can tell her I'm in the A.L.A. But maybe it's a bit too soon for that now."

"Guido has a better idea. He wonders whether we could recruit her. What do you think?"

"You mean Mona join the organization?"

"Yes."

"Wow! That's fantastic. It would solve all my problems."

"We're not thinking about *your* problems, Paul. We're thinking about the organization."

"Of course."

"We need a smart young woman on the team," Chucky said. "For a special project we're working on."

"What project is that?" asked Paul.

"I'm sorry, but I can't tell you. Not yet."

"O.K. I understand."

"Will you ask her if she wants to join?"

"Yes," said Paul. "I'll ask her tonight."

*   *   *

The main course at supper consisted of a casserole in which all kinds of salvaged leftovers and scraps were put to use. Mrs. MacVicar, under the delusion that there was something Italian about this dish, called it Scrapolini. But despite this brave effort at fantasy in nomenclature, Scrapolini inevitably elicited some of the boarders' most bitter comments.

"What is this, Mrs. MacVicar?" said Bud Sorenson, picking something off his plate. "Is it a goat hair?"

"Definitely not, Mr. Sorenson," said Mrs. MacVicar. "It might be a bit of silk from a corn husk, that's all."

"Christ, I think I've just eaten an eyeball," said Spiro Costakis.

"You wouldn't believe how well we Anglos used to eat, before Separation," said Mr. Brophy. "At home, every Sunday night, we used to have a big roast of beef—a standing rib, we used to call it. With Yorkshire pudding and Idaho potatoes. And I would preside over it with my electric carving knife."

"You were master in your own house," said Sorenson.

"That's right. We were *maîtres chez nous*."

Paul tried to catch Mona's eye, across the table, but she was deep in conversation with Doreen Brewster. This had been going on all through the meal.

"If you had roast beef every week," said Lionel Greenspoon, "it was because you were exploiting the French. We Anglos are now paying for that exploitation. Don't tell me the French had roast beef too."

"They had their pork pies and their pickled beets," said Mr. Brophy. "They were perfectly happy with that."

After dinner, the boarders all went into the parlour, where a brief party was being held in honour of Colin Armitage, who was being expelled from Mrs. MacVicar's. Bud Sorenson had volunteered to pour a shot of De Kuyper's Gin for everybody, so that Armitage could be given a proper send-off.

"Ladies and gentlemen," Sorenson said, after filling the glasses, "we are gathered here tonight to say farewell to a worthy colleague, a man who has shared with us the worst that can be offered by this foul slum in which we are forced to live. We have had our differences with Colin, but basically he is one of us, a wretched victim of Mrs. MacVicar's oppression. I wish she was here right now, in this room, so that we could tell her what a rotten thing she has done by throwing Colin out into the street.

"But perhaps it is more fitting that we put aside our disgust for a moment and think more positively. So let us raise our glasses and toast Colin Armitage. Let us wish him good luck in all his future enterprises, and courage to face whatever horrors may await him at his next boarding house, if he is able to find one."

"To Colin Armitage," said the boarders, raising their glasses and drinking.

"Oh, Colin, I feel so awful," said Doreen Brewster, a tear

rolling down her cheek. "I wish I'd signed your petition, I really do."

"Yes, sorry about that," said Spiro Costakis.

"Speech, speech!" said Mr. Brophy.

Armitage, who was wearing his raincoat and had his cardboard suitcase with him, downed his drink and cleared his throat.

"Ladies and gentlemen," he said, "I am deeply touched by this gesture of yours. I sometimes used to think that you all despised me because of my problem, but now I know otherwise. Because of your send-off, I leave this rat-trap without bitterness. I knew the rules and I broke them, and that's that. As you all know, I was caught this afternoon using Mrs. Mac-Vicar's own private bathroom, and now I am paying the penalty.

"But I was in that bathroom for forty-five minutes before she caught me, and during that time I had some very deep thoughts, even some revelations. We all know that the French have forced us into economic degradation, making it almost impossible for us to eat properly or to make love. But they have robbed us even further than that. They have taken from us even the simple enjoyment of nature's most basic bodily function. We have reached the point – "

"Just a minute, just a minute!" said Lionel Greenspoon. "It's not the French who keep us from having a decent bowel movement. It's Mrs. MacVicar and all the other Anglo landladies. We can't blame the French for every bloody misfortune we bring on ourselves."

"Oh no?" said Armitage. "Then how come the French can blame the Anglos for everything that ever went wrong for *them*, all through history? How come they don't blame their own Church, which is what really screwed them up? Everybody knows it was the Church that turned them all into priests and notaries, while the Anglos were becoming businessmen and accumulating money. It was their own Church that kept them poor and ignorant for two hundred years, but they blame

125

us for it. In that case, I can blame *them* for my constipation. If they didn't make me so poor, I would have a toilet of my own."

"Hear, hear!" said Spiro Costakis.

"Maybe some day you *will* have a toilet of your own, Colin," said Doreen Brewster.

"That's what I wanted to say before I was interrupted," said Armitage. "It all became clear to me this afternoon, during those blessed forty-five minutes, before I was caught. Some day, I thought to myself, we Anglos will rise up, and win for ourselves the right to properly sit down! May that day not be too far off, comrades! God bless you all, and when we meet again let it be on the barricades!"

"Jesus," said Greenspoon, nervously, "do you want to get us all arrested?"

"Don't worry, Greenspoon," said Sorenson, "there are no spies here, unless it's you yourself."

"That was a beautiful speech, Colin," said Mr. Brophy, shaking Armitage's hand.

"Where are you going to live?" said Costakis. "I hope you're not going to have to sleep in the park."

"No, I'm in luck," said Armitage. "There's a bed that just became free at Mrs. Bannister's, down the street."

"That *is* luck."

"Yes, it's the bed of a fellow I know, but it just happens that he was expelled from it yesterday. For fornication."

As the boarders sipped their gin, Paul drew Mona aside. "I have to speak to you," he said. "It's important."

"I'm sorry," said Mona. "I can't spare the time."

"I want to tell you where I really was that night. And last night and the night before."

"Are you going to tell the truth?"

"Yes. Please believe me, Mona. I'm going to tell the truth."

"All right. Let's go upstairs."

Mona's roommate was out. Mona sat down on the edge of her bed and looked up at Paul tensely, as though expecting bad news.

"I've become a Separatist," Paul said. "I've joined the Anglo Liberation Army. That's where I've been these nights."

"Is that where they're holding the chess tournament?" she said.

"It wasn't true, about the chess tournament. But this *is* true."

"Then why didn't you tell me?"

"I wanted to, but I couldn't. It had to be kept secret, until I could get permission to tell you, from my commanding officer."

"Why should I believe you, Paul?"

"Because it's true."

She got up from the bed and came over to him. She looked into his eyes for some time. "You know," she finally said, "I think you *are* telling the truth."

"I am."

"Do you realize how hurt I was when you walked out of this room on Thursday night?"

"I know. I suffered too."

They put their arms around each other and embraced for a long time, in silence.

"What's it like," she asked, "to be in the A.L.A.? It must be very exciting."

"It is, Mona. Especially to know that we're fighting for something so worthwhile. Think of it—a country of our own, with our own flag and our own government. A country where Anglos can regain their pride and hold their heads high."

"Paul, I'm proud of you."

"It'll be a democracy, Mona."

"I'm ashamed of the terrible thoughts I've been having about you, the last few days."

"Half of the Island of Montreal and part of the Eastern Townships. It'll be a beautiful country."

"I thought you were chasing after women, but you've been fighting for your people."

"English will be the official language."

"I envy you, Paul. I'm just drifting through life, but you're *doing* something."

"I thought you were going to escape to the States. You'll be doing something there, won't you – achieving something?"

"Maybe. But it's running away, isn't it? Isn't it cowardly?"

"Then why don't you join the A.L.A.? Become one of us. Fight for separation from Quebec."

Again she looked at him for a long time without speaking. Then she said, "Yes, I would like to do that. Very much."

"That's great. I really hoped you'd say that."

They embraced and sank down on the bed, their mouths locked together in a hungry kiss. Paul slipped his hand under her sweater and caressed the smoothness of her back.

"It's Thursday," Mona murmured. "Mrs. MacVicar is out. Cathy is out."

He put his hand under her skirt and felt the warmth of her thighs. At last it was going to happen. But suddenly he stopped.

"We can't," he said. "I just remembered."

"What?"

"There's a meeting of the cell tonight. In just half an hour from now. I'm supposed to bring you, if you want to join."

* * *

When they arrived at the meeting place, the woman called Margaret took Mona aside, into an empty room, and searched her for hidden radio transmitters or homing devices. This came as a relief to Paul, who had been worried that the search might have taken place in front of everybody.

When Margaret and Mona emerged from the room, Mona still wearing her blindfold, she was asked why she wanted to join the A.L.A.

"I believe in the cause," she said. "I've only realized that recently. Also, I have to say I feel very guilty about my work. You see, I'm a seamstress at *l'Atelier national du costume*, and I guess the costumes I sew there all help to further French nationalism. My joining this organization will help set things right."

128

"Take her blindfold off," said Guido. "And congratulations, Mona, you're one of us now."

"Thank you," said Mona.

"I have an announcement," said Guido. "I can now reveal that our most important activity during the twentieth anniversary celebrations will be something called Operation Thunderbolt. So far, only three of us know all the details, and I can't tell the rest of you very much about it until you absolutely have to know. Just in case you're captured and interrogated.

"I can say, however, that Operation Thunderbolt, if successful, will bring us a very large amount of money. Enough to send a small delegation to Europe to buy arms and ammunition. We'll also set up a small office in London, to tell the world how Quebec oppresses its Anglos, and to gain support for the new country we are going to create – a free and independent Angloland."

"Wait a minute, Guido," said Chucky. "You know very well that some of us want to call it New Canada. I think you should mention that the name hasn't been officially decided yet."

"All right, all right," said Guido, "the name hasn't been decided. But let's get back to Operation Thunderbolt. Some of you – but not all of you – are going to be involved in the actual operation. But I want all of you to be on stand-by from the twentieth of June to the twenty-sixth, inclusive. We may call on you at any time, and you must be prepared to risk your lives."

12

It was now June, and the twentieth anniversary celebrations were under way. This was the month when French workers would have their twenty-one paid holidays and the Anglos would have their nine. Throughout Montreal, great blue-and-white banners stretched from one side of the street to the other. *VIVE LE QUÉBEC LIBRE!* said some of them. Others said *VINGT ANS DE LIBERTÉ* or *VINGT ANS DE JUSTICE*. Any Anglo caught removing or defacing these assertions was liable to six months in prison.

Walking along Wellington Street, after supper, Mona and Paul found that the banners did nothing to enliven this melancholy thoroughfare. If anything, the strollers looked more listless and more dejected than ever. Some seemed almost catatonic as they stood gazing at the dimly-lit pawnshop windows, at battered tea kettles and second-hand toilet seats.

"Why do Anglos have to be so *drab*?" Mona said. "Why do we never show any spirit, any gaiety?"

"Because we're an oppressed people," Paul said. "But all that will change when we have a country of our own. Then we'll be full of joy and vitality."

"How come the French were so lively before they had *their* own country? How come they had all that theatre and music when they were still part of Canada?"

"That's because they didn't have any real troubles. At least not compared with us today."

"I don't know. I think maybe we Anglos are a fundamentally gloomy people."

They walked on, hand in hand, past the horsemeat butcher's and past the public baths and de-lousing station.

"I wonder what this Operation Thunderbolt is going to be?" Mona said.

"I don't know," said Paul, "but I think you're going to be involved."

"What makes you think that?"

"Last week, before you joined, Chucky told me they needed a bright young woman for a special project."

"And you think that's me?"

"Yes, I think so."

"It sounds kind of scary, doesn't it?"

"Yes, I guess it does."

"Do you think you'll be in on it too?" Mona asked. "Guido said only some of us would be involved."

"I certainly hope so," Paul said. "It would be much better if we were in it together, don't you think?"

"Yes."

They continued along Wellington Street, pausing for a moment to join a small crowd outside the second-hand mattress shop. In honour of the twentieth anniversary all mattresses that were more than twenty years old were being auctioned off at bargain prices. For Paul, the sight of these mattresses brought on a sharp pang of desire. How he would love to be stretched out on one of them, no matter how lumpy, with Mona at his side. Would that *ever* come to pass? How long could they go on this way, aching for a chance to consummate their love? Tonight, once again, it would be impossible, and they would have to settle for frustrated kissing and caressing on their favourite bench, in Marguerite Bourgeoys Park.

But when they got there, an unpleasant surprise awaited them. The park was no longer dark. The lights that had once been extinguished by Anglo slingshots had all been replaced, with bulbs that were brighter than ever. Between the trees banners proclaimed *VINGT ANS DE RÉCRÉATION PUBLIQUE* and *VINGT*

ANS D'AIR PUR. Loudspeakers had been put up, and from them, at great volume, came the hallowed refrains of Gilles Vigneault and Pauline Julien.

In normal times each bench in the park would accommodate up to three Anglo couples, all embracing passionately in the dark. But tonight most of the benches were unoccupied. Members of the Recreation Police patrolled the footpaths, to make sure that no one shot out the lights. But none of the usual volunteer patrolmen from the Presbyterian Vigilance League were on hand, for there was no longer any need for them; under these bright lights, the mildest kind of necking was barely feasible, and even the most pessimistic moralist would have to admit that there was no danger whatever of an outbreak of fornication.

From the loudspeakers, there came a hoarse song, with guitar accompaniment:

> *Ma ville c'est ben frette,*
> *La neige tombe toujours...*

"They're really rubbing our noses in it, aren't they, with that music?" said Paul.

> *Mais la chose qui me chauffe,*
> *C'est l'indépendance.*

It was a song by Raoul Renaud, a fast-rising young *chansonnier*. Government sociologists had determined that this song was third in national popularity, and this entitled Renaud to wear two chevrons on the sleeve of his white satin blouse.

> *C'était l'esclavage,*
> *Dans un pays ben triste...*

"This used to be *our* park," Mona said, "and now they've taken that away from us too."

"We've got to change all this," said Paul.

"We will," said Mona.

"Do you want to sit down?"

"No, let's go home. This place gives me the creeps."

Victoire extraordinaire
Pour la culture majoritaire.

* * *

Back at Mrs. MacVicar's, in the parlour, the boarders were sitting around the ten-inch television set. As Mona and Paul joined them, the Minister of Information came on the screen, introducing a major documentary film that had been made for the twentieth anniversary.

The Minister was a familiar face on television; he was on at least twice a week, to point out to the people of Quebec that they had never been happier, thanks to the arrival of the Post-Industrial Age. The promulgation of this notion kept the Minister very busy, although his main task was to protect the collectivity from alien ideologies that might threaten its aspirations. Thus he and the sociologists on his staff spent a good deal of time thinking up ways to prevent the Québécois people from learning what was going on across the sealed border, in the United States. It would only confuse them to know that their cousins in the State of Ontario and the State of New Brunswick owned automobiles, washing machines, sixteen-track stereo systems and ninety-six channel television sets.

In Quebec, there was only one channel. And there was only one kind of television set for sale, a highly-simplified brown box that was designed to pick up that one channel and nothing else. Only older Quebeckers remembered the days when you could choose between many Canadian and American programs. Now, of course, picking up stations located across the border was impossible. But, even so, the Minister of Information never tired of denouncing the unseen American shows: they were obscene, violent, materialistic and – worst of all – they were in the English language.

The documentary that Mrs. MacVicar's boarders were watching dealt with agriculture in Quebec. "...*le défi d'une*

133

vie nouvelle... " the narrator was saying, as the camera showed fifty or so families boarding a train in Montreal. They were on their way north, to the Abitibi region. There, along with a few hundred thousand other former factory workers, they were being resettled on farms.

"Poor buggers," said Bud Sorenson. "I feel sorry for them."

"What makes you think they're not happy?" said Lionel Greenspoon, defending the government, as usual. "Maybe they feel sorry for *you*, stuck here in this crowded city."

"I bet they wish they had a choice," said Sorenson.

After the train left the station, the documentary moved on to discuss new developments in the field of urban agriculture. It showed a large number of labourers at work with pickaxes, breaking up a wide expanse of pavement. This had once been a parking lot for automobiles, in downtown Montreal.

"In colonial times," the narrator said, "this pavement reeked of deadly gasoline fumes. But grass will soon grow here again, as it did in 1642, when the first brave Québécois settlers arrived from France. Once again, cows will graze here, and sheep, and goats. Once again, city and country will blend together, in the healthy ecology of three hundred years ago."

The documentary now began a montage of artistic close-ups of pickaxes, sledgehammers, and the sweaty torsos of the Anglo labourers who wielded them. As they worked, the labourers sang "Men of Harlech," having received permission to do so from the Folklore Licensing Board.

"Cows downtown," said Sorenson. "Now I've heard everything."

"What gets me," said Costakis, "is how the French can swallow all this crap – that this post-industrial society, as they call it, is something they're doing on purpose."

"Small is beautiful," Greenspoon said. "But I don't suppose you guys can understand that. But the fact is, we don't have to worship bigness any more, for its own sake. We don't have to breathe polluted air and drink poisoned water. Instead, Quebec is developing what is called 'appropriate technology.' In this

134

country, the age of the machine is over."

"It's over because they fucked it up with their crazy politics," said Sorenson. "And their crazy language laws."

"I still don't understand why the French stand for it," said Costakis. "They're so bloody much poorer than they were when they were part of Canada."

"Yes," said Sorenson, "but even though the French of Quebec have managed to impoverish themselves, the Linguistic Purity Laws make it certain that the Anglos will be even poorer than they are. Thus the sociologists tell us that we Anglos are now fourteen per cent poorer than the French. And that's the essence of nationalism – to have somebody *underneath* you, even if it's not very far underneath."

"Sorenson, you're a racist," said Greenspoon.

"What do you mean, a racist?"

"The way you keep attacking the French. The way you belittle them."

"I'm attacking their politics, not their race."

"You make fun of their efforts to establish their own language in their own country. Language is a racial attribute. Therefore you're a racist, pure and simple."

"Language is more ethnic than racial, isn't it?" said Mr. Brophy.

"I think it has more to do with culture than with ethnicity," said Mona.

"Maybe you could say it's ethnocultural," said Paul.

"Look, Greenspoon," said Sorenson, "I can't be a racist against the French because they're not a race. A race is either black, white, brown or yellow."

"The French are white, aren't they?" said Greenspoon.

"Of course. That means a black person who hates a Frenchman is a racist, and so is a Chinese. But a white Anglo can't be a racist vis-à-vis the French because he's hating within his own colour, if you know what I mean."

"What would you call him then, if he isn't a racist?"

"Call him a political adversary."

135

"A member of an oppressed minority," said Doreen.

"An underdog," said Mr. Brophy.

"That's right, an underdog."

"Hey, look at that," Doreen said, pointing at the television screen. "I think they're going to make love."

The documentary had left the parking-lot pasture and now showed two small animals in a cage, sniffing each other. This was taking place in the former Queen Elizabeth Hotel, which had been converted into an experimental mink ranch.

* * *

Chucky and Guido were discussing strategy.

"I had a report from Kevin this morning," Guido said. "He thinks June twenty-third will probably be the date."

"But we can't be sure, can we?" Chucky said.

"No, probably not until the last minute."

"When can we let the others in on the plan? They're all very anxious to know."

"We can tell them at the next meeting."

"Good. Will Kevin be there?" Chucky asked.

"He's going to try to make it."

"How do you think Mona will get along with Kevin?"

"She'd *better* get along with him. This whole Operation Thunderbolt is going to depend on the two of them."

"I wish Kevin wasn't such a cocksman," Chucky said. "He's going to try to get into her pants for sure."

"He'll probably succeed, won't he?"

"Well, they say women can't resist him."

"If it'll make him and Mona work well together, so much the better," said Guido.

"Yes, but I still feel like a rat, doing this to poor old Paul."

"This is no time to be sentimental, Chucky. Remember what Mao Tse-tung said: 'A revolution is not a dinner party.'"

13

Kevin O'Donnell sat in the airport departure lounge, eating the sandwich he had brought for lunch. As he ate, he looked out the big window and watched the Tarom jet lumber down the runway. It picked up speed and took off, soaring up over the foothills of the Laurentians. Soon it would turn in a great arc and head eastward, toward Europe.

Kevin wondered what it would be like to fly with Tarom, the Romanian airline. Their food, he had heard, was superb, but their safety record was somewhat spotty. Still, he would rather take his chances with Tarom than with the Albanian airline, or Air Zaire. But, come to think of it, he would fly with *any* of them, if only he had the chance. Anything to get out of Quebec.

But that opportunity would be coming soon, wouldn't it? If Operation Thunderbolt worked as planned – and it *would* – Kevin would be one of the members of the Anglo Liberation Army who would be heading for London, with large suitcases full of money. It would be the first time he had ever flown.

He finished his sandwich and glanced at his watch. The flight he was waiting for should be arriving in about fifteen minutes. He brushed a few crumbs from his uniform and went downstairs to the chauffeurs' waiting-room, next to the V.I.P. Lounge.

There were fourteen other chauffeurs there, all of them wearing the elegant livery of the Government of Quebec drivers' pool. Their knee-high boots were of glistening black leather and their tunics and breeches were powder blue, a colour that harmonized nicely with the royal blue of the official electrocars they drove.

"*Bonjour tout le monde*," Kevin said, as he entered the waiting-room.

"*Salut, Kevin*," said three or four of the chauffeurs. Although Kevin was an Anglo – in fact the only Anglo in the drivers' pool – he was accepted as an equal by his colleagues, and they willingly shared with him the jokes, gossip, and complaints of their trade.

Kevin walked across the waiting-room and entered the washroom, to examine himself in the mirror. As he suspected, there was a small smudge of lipstick on the collar of his tunic. From his pocket he took the tiny bottle of spot remover he always carried; he moistened his handkerchief with the fluid and started dabbing away at his collar. As he did so, he examined his eyes in the mirror. They looked the way they felt – slightly bloodshot. Well, there was good reason for this: last night Marie-Thérèse had been at her most insatiable and he had been able to get precious little sleep.

His cheeks looked tired too, if that was possible. He felt a twinge of anxiety as he started wondering, once again, whether he was beginning to show signs of age. A few years ago, a night of white wine and gymnastics with Marie-Thérèse would have had almost no effect at all on his energies of the next day. But now, at the age of twenty-eight, there was no doubt that it took him a little while longer to bounce back after a heavy night.

Thank God, Kevin thought, that Marie-Thérèse's husband was coming back to town today, so there was no question of another night of the death-defying acrobatics so dear to her heart.

He finished expunging the last traces of lipstick from his collar and went back into the chauffeurs' waiting-room. Here he found his colleagues clustered around the bulletin board, reading a notice that had just been posted. It was their work schedule for the month of June, during the twentieth anniversary celebrations.

"How can they ask us to be on call sixteen hours a day, every day?" one of the chauffeurs was saying.

"They're not asking us, they're telling us," said another.

"It's really going to be rough."

"Yes, but what about all that overtime pay? I can certainly use that."

"I can use some rest."

"And think of the tips. Those foreign delegations aren't afraid to throw their money around."

"Are you kidding? Did you ever get a tip from a Russian? Or a Bulgarian?"

"I'm thinking of the Africans, not the Europeans. The Africans are true gentlemen."

"Well, you may have a point there."

"They're really going to keep us hopping. I hear there'll be as many as five planes a day coming in."

"Five planes a day? You must be dreaming."

"I'm serious. You wait and see."

The usual traffic at Mirabel Airport consisted of two arrivals and two departures a day. European airlines, such as Air France, Aeroflot, Malev, Lot and Tarom each came and went once a week, while the African lines, such as Air Senegal and Air Togo, came once a fortnight. As for Air Quebec, it had one flight a week to Europe, one flight every two weeks to Africa, and one a month to the Far East. It accomplished all this with the one and only plane it had that was capable of intercontinental flight, an aging Ilyushin 371.

"Five planes a day? Who's going to be *on* them?"

"All the people who are coming for the anniversary. Delegations, sports teams, scholars, scientists, journalists, television crews, movie stars – everybody."

"All packed into that broken-down Ilyushin of ours?"

"All the airlines are putting on extra flights. And Air Quebec is renting two big American jets from Air Nicaragua. They'll be painted blue and white for the occasion and we'll have them all month."

Kevin looked out the window into the sky. In the distance the Air Quebec flight could be seen approaching, on time for once. He left the chauffeurs' waiting-room and went out to the arrivals concourse, where he watched the television crews setting up their equipment.

As usual, there were three crews on hand, waiting for the plane. In Quebec, as in most Third World countries, television newscasts never carried any bad news; thus there was much broadcast time to fill, and this was devoted to exhaustive coverage of the arrival and departure of visiting dignitaries. Today's airport arrivals, being recorded for tonight's newscast, would include a delegation of East German sugar-beet experts and a Cambodian basketball team. And, of course, there would be the usual fifteen or twenty returning Quebec cabinet ministers and senior civil servants. It was one of these – the Minister of Tourism, Fish and Game – that Kevin O'Donnell was waiting for.

In the new Quebec, high government officials were always on the go, although the ordinary citizen had little hope of ever setting foot outside the country. Still, the people did not begrudge their officials their globe-trotting perquisites. They were proud to think that Quebec was represented at so many international congresses and festivals of the arts. And, if a cabinet minister needed a few days at the beach, to unwind after a particularly gruelling festival, surely that was not too much to ask; it was little enough recompense for the onus of having to decide, day after day, what was best for the Quebec "collectivity." Now that that collectivity had been relieved of the onerous burden of voting, it was all the more important that decisions be made by officials who were relaxed and clear-headed.

In the old days, Quebec's rulers used to take their ease in Miami in the winter or at Old Orchard Beach, Maine, in the summer. But the closing of the American border now kept them away from these beloved haunts, and so they had to venture farther afield. In the summer they went to Varna and Ma-

maia, on the Black Sea, and to Sopot, on the Baltic; in the winter they were to be found on the beaches of Dakar, or around the blissful swimming pool of the Hotel Ivoire in Abidjan.

President Chartrand encouraged his ministers to travel. It was he himself who actually made all the important decisions in Quebec, and he didn't like having too many members of his cabinet in the country at any one time; the more of them that were in town the more bother it was for the President, who was forever being called upon to settle their petty squabbles.

The first arriving passengers were now coming through the door and Kevin watched the camera crew filming the bewildered-looking Cambodian basketball team. It was at moments like this, when passengers were arriving from abroad, that Kevin felt his most acute pangs of envy. These people had danced in the discotheques of London and had sipped Pernod in the cafés of the Champs Elysées. But, above all, they had driven fast cars – real automobiles that ran on gasoline. The government electrocar that Kevin drove had a top speed of seventy-five kilometres an hour, but these East German sugar-beet men, now being interviewed at great length by one of the television crews, had driven motorcars that could easily do 150 kilometres an hour, or even 200.

For a Montreal Anglo, a trip to Europe was as unlikely as a trip to Saturn, but Kevin would soon be on his way, in the grand culmination of Operation Thunderbolt. And he would not be coming back to Quebec. Instead, he would be staying in London, helping to set up the A.L.A.'s first office abroad, to buy arms and ammunition and to spread the word about the oppression of the Anglos of Montreal. That would mean travelling a great deal, all over Europe. Kevin would do that in a real, gasoline-driven automobile.

The last passengers from the Air Quebec flight were now coming out of customs and into the arrivals concourse. The Minister of Tourism, Suzanne Levasseur, was among them, and Kevin went over to greet her. She was a tall, handsome woman of forty, dressed in the best that Paris had to offer. She was

141

accompanied by two porters, carrying her many suitcases.

"*Bonjour, madame,*" Kevin said.

"*Ah, Kevin!*" she said. "*Quelle belle surprise! Je ne savais pas que ce serait toi qui me conduirais.*"

"*Je suis très content d'être à votre service, madame.*"

He guided her toward the blue electrocar and opened the door for her. Then he supervised the porters, stowing her luggage in the trunk. When this was done, he walked around to the right fender and unfurled the little blue *fleur-de-lys* flag that signified the presence of a minister of state in the car.

"How has the weather been?" Suzanne Levasseur said, as they drove off from the airport.

"It has been very fine, madame," said Kevin.

"For goodness sake, will you stop calling me 'madame?'"

"I'm just trying to be correct," Kevin said.

"After all, we used to sleep together, didn't we?"

"Yes, but that was a long time ago."

"Only a year ago, Kevin."

Kevin reached up and adjusted the rear-view mirror, so he could see her, sitting there in the back seat. She was smiling, in her faintly cynical way, and she looked marvellous. She was wearing her hair longer than she used to and, as she reached up to smooth it back with a slim, gloved hand, he remembered what an elegant person she was. There was a great serenity about her, in sharp contrast to the earthy, hyperactive Marie-Thérèse.

"What have you been doing with yourself, Kevin?" she said. "Still consoling the wives of cabinet ministers?"

"What on earth do you mean?"

"You know very well what I mean. You drive the minister and his wife to the airport and then, after she says goodbye to him, you drive her home – and she invites you in."

"That's never happened to me, Suzanne."

"I hear you have been offering comfort to Marie-Thérèse Bolduc, while Pierre has been at the United Nations."

"Where did you hear that?"

"Gossip."

"It's completely untrue."

"Then who is it, these days? You must be making *someone* happy."

"No one, Suzanne. I live the life of a monk."

"I'll bet you do."

"Honestly."

"I'm disappointed with you, Kevin. You ought to be able to do better than La Bolduc. You know what they call her, don't you?"

"No, what?"

"They call her 'the chauffeur's friend.' You're not the first, you know. Marie-Thérèse has delved quite deeply into the drivers' pool."

Suzanne was smiling now and Kevin remembered the tactics she had used, when they were lovers, on those occasions when she suspected him of having other women. She never displayed anger or possessiveness; she simply teased him and managed to make him feel ridiculous.

Kevin's affair with Suzanne Levasseur had lasted for eight months. When it started, he was just another aging Anglo delivery boy, bringing groceries to her apartment. After his third delivery she had asked him to stay for coffee.

"Perhaps you can teach me some English," she had said. "I have often thought that a few words in your language would come in handy when I'm visiting Europe." Like most French Quebeckers, she had never had any dealings with Anglos, either professionally or socially. There had only been the usual fleeting contacts with Anglo maids, laundry workers or shoe repairmen.

After they went to bed for the first time, Suzanne told him that she had never experienced anything like it before. Two weeks later she procured a Certificate of Linguistic Purity for him, without his having to take the examination. Soon after that she helped him land this well-paying job as a government chauffeur.

During their time together, Suzanne had been a senior civil servant, not yet a cabinet minister. When she called a halt to the affair, she did it with admirable honesty. "I'm very ambitious, Kevin," she said. "I'm being considered for the Cabinet, but I'll never get it if the President finds out I'm involved with an Anglo." And so they went their separate ways, and in the year that had passed since then he had been assigned to act as her chauffeur on only one other occasion.

Kevin's regrets at breaking up with Suzanne had been tempered by his interest, at the time, in a girl called Danielle, whom he had just met. Danielle had an astonishing figure and, as it turned out, she was very available. But now, looking at Suzanne through his rear-view mirror, Kevin realized that none of the women he had ever slept with had anything like the charm and style of this minister of state.

"How was Paris?" Kevin said.

"Beautiful as usual," Suzanne said. "But it's strange how one can love France and at the same time despise the French."

"That's a common reaction, isn't it?"

"They're so condescending. They don't seem to have any gratitude to Quebec for preserving their language in North America."

"But they're always ready to send over a theatre company, or a cultural delegation."

"Yes, but they won't send money. And that's what Quebec needs – money."

The foreign policy of France had never been noted for altruism or sentimentality, but in its relations with Quebec the Quai d'Orsay outdid itself in its display of unadorned self-interest. In fact France seemed indecently anxious to comply with the wishes of the United States, which kept asking its allies not to extend material assistance of any kind to "Cuba North." This American policy originated with the powerful bloc of Canadian senators in the United States Congress, a group of men deter-

144

mined to prove that Quebec could not survive as an independent state.

"It's tragic," Suzanne said, "to think that the United States means more to France than Quebec does."

"Well," Kevin said, "the Americans buy an awful lot of French wine."

"Thank God for the Russians and the Africans. I don't know what we'd do without them."

Kevin drove the smooth, silent electrocar along Boulevard de Maisonneuve. When he reached Le Parizeau, he drove down its ramp into the underground garage, where several other government electrocars were parked. Before Separation, Le Parizeau had been known as Westmount Square. It had been designed by Mies van der Rohe, and in its heyday it was one of Montreal's most elegant and opulent apartment buildings. It was now starting to show signs of wear, but it was still one of the best addresses in town; the Anglo tycoons who used to live here had been flushed out long ago, and now it was the preserve of cabinet ministers, army generals, and sociologists of the highest rank.

Kevin took the suitcases from the trunk of the electrocar and carried them into the elevator. Suzanne was smiling faintly at him, as though still teasing, as they went up to the seventeenth floor.

"I don't think you've been here since the apartment was redone," she said, as he carried the bags in.

"No, I haven't. It looks great."

"You get a complete redecoration job when they make you a cabinet minister," she said. "The wallpaper is from Spain."

"Beautiful."

"Would you like a drink?"

"That would be very nice."

"Pour yourself one, would you please? You know where it is. And a Cinzano for me. I'm just going to change. I'll be back in a minute."

She went down the hall towards the bedroom, and he poured

the drinks at the sideboard. Then, as he sipped his Scotch, he wandered around the vast living-room, looking at the new furniture. It was more sumptuous than anything he had ever seen before – a fabulous array of chrome, lucite, rosewood, and rich brown leather.

He went to the picture window and looked out at the view of the city. Below, to the south and the west, was the sombre grey expanse of the Anglo slums. Beyond that was the wide blue swath of the St. Lawrence River. And in the middle of the river was Ile des Soeurs (Nuns' Island), where the long rows of townhouses and barracks-like apartment buildings had been converted into one of the country's biggest political re-education centres. It was here that dissenters were housed until they could convince the authorities that they had seen the error of their ways.

At the far end of Nuns' Island was the maximum-security jail where sixteen members of the Anglo Liberation Army were believed to be incarcerated. If Operation Thunderbolt failed, Kevin and a few others from the General Wolfe Cell might be joining them.

This thought brought on a pang of anxiety and once again he started reviewing the scheme in his mind, looking for its weak points. For instance, what about this Mona Rosenstein? Would she really be able to carry off her end of it, which was very tricky? So much would depend on her. He hadn't met her yet, and she didn't know yet just what was required of her. He hoped Guido and Chucky were right when they said she was perfect for this dangerous assignment.

But he must think positively. The plan was a sound one. It would go like clockwork and before the end of June he would be in London. Life there would be very pleasant, if only his companions were sensible about it. He was thinking of the other guerrillas who would be going with him, on this A.L.A. mission. He hoped they wouldn't be excessively gung-ho; he hoped they wouldn't want to live in some unheated garret, and cook their own meals, so they could spend as much of that

146

Thunderbolt money as possible on guns and dynamite. He hoped they would realize that revolutionaries couldn't live by guns alone.

Kevin didn't see himself in London as just another hollow-cheeked Anglo bomb-thrower. He would be much more valuable to the cause as a suave young diplomat, an ambassador for a country-to-be. As such he would need a luxurious flat in Mayfair. And that automobile he would drive might as well be a Maserati. Yes, he saw himself behind the wheel of a bullet-like Maserati, hurtling down the Autostrada toward Rome, where he would be giving an important press conference. On the seat beside him would be a glorious blonde, long-legged and as exciting as the Maserati itself.

"It's still a wonderful view of the city, isn't it?" said Suzanne, who had just come back into the room. She had changed from her travelling clothes into blue jeans.

"Yes, it's a terrific view," Kevin said.

"But the building itself is going to the dogs," Suzanne said. "There are a lot of undesirables moving in."

"I thought you had to be pretty important to get in here."

"Yes, you do. Maybe it's just that the wrong kind of people are becoming important. The new Admiral of the Fleet just moved in, down the hall. He's always drunk and once he tried to grab hold of me."

"I hear there are a lot more sociologists living here now," Kevin said.

"Yes, and they're the worst. They're so full of their own importance. They elbow right past you to get into the elevator."

"You never did like sociologists, did you?"

"I detest them," Suzanne said. "But I suppose they're a necessary evil."

In the new Quebec, bright young men who would once have gone into the priesthood now became sociologists instead, but their training provided them with nothing that resembled ecclesiastical humility. They were, in fact, quite arrogant, knowing full well that they were essential to the operation of what President Chartrand called "guided democracy." In this form of government, the state no longer tried to ascertain the desires of the people through the crude, unscientific method of elections, held only once every four or five years. Now, instead, there were surveys, polls and referendums, carried out with great frequency by the government's sociologists. In this way, the President said, the government was always "fine-tuned" to the wishes of the people.

Malcontents might suspect that the sociologists cooked the books so as to give the President whatever results he wanted, from any given survey, but loyalists staunchly maintained that the referendum was the only true form of democracy. Also, surveys and polls provided valuable clues as to which citizens required political re-education. At the moment, for instance, the cells on Nuns' Island were full of people who, when recently questioned by sociologists, failed to express sufficient alarm at the dangers threatening the survival of the French language in Quebec.

"It's like old times, you and me here like this," Suzanne said. She was standing beside Kevin, at the window, her glass of Cinzano in her hand.

"Just like old times," Kevin said.

"You look tired, Kevin," she said. "Perhaps it's too much Marie-Thérèse."

"I don't know what you're talking about."

"Is it true that she has a trampoline in her bedroom, and mirrors on the ceiling?"

"Actually," said Kevin, "she has a flying trapeze, like in the circus. And there's no net underneath. If you fall off, you've had it."

"She has made you so tired, the wicked woman," Suzanne said. "Look at these circles under your eyes." She put her Cinzano down and touched Kevin's face. As she did so, she looked up at him, her lips moist and waiting. He put his arms around her and they kissed.

"Maybe you're too tired," she said.

"Well," Kevin said, "I've been driving a lot, but I'm not too tired."

They kissed again, long and deep.

"Do you remember the things I used to do with my tongue?" she asked.

"Yes."

"But does *he* remember?" she said, slowly reaching down to his zipper. "Does he remember how I used to wake him up when he was sleepy?"

And, as they kissed, the Minister of Tourism, Fish and Game gently opened the fly of Kevin's powder-blue chauffeur's breeches.

14

"The title of my article is 'Bitter Medicine,'" Margaret said. She took a sheaf of paper from her handbag, put on her glasses, and started to read:

"Why are so many of the world's people eager to learn English? And why do so many people want to avoid speaking French? What is it that makes English such a sweet elixir, and French such a bitter medicine?"

Margaret paused and looked up at the members of the General Wolfe Cell of the Anglo Liberation Army. She was pleased to see that they were listening more attentively to her article than to the one that Robert, the scholarly young guerrilla, had just finished reading. Robert had written a rather boring speculation about what Che Guevara might have accomplished had he been born a Montreal Anglo. Both Robert's and Margaret's articles were being considered for publication in *The Liberator*, the A.L.A.'s underground newspaper.

Margaret resumed her reading. "We Anglos have many potential allies outside Quebec," she said, "who are just as anxious as we are to have no more of this bitter French medicine shoved down their throats. France itself is teeming with such people. In Brittany, the people wânt to speak Breton, not French. The Basques want to speak Basque, not French. The Corsicans want to speak their Italian dialect, not French. The people of Roussillon want to speak Catalan, not French. The people of Languedoc want to speak Provençal, not French.

"What makes French the language of coercion? What makes

it so cordially detested by all those non-French people who are forced to do business in it? Can it be the irregular verbs that are at the heart of this troublesome language? Look, for instance, at the verb *aller*. If there were any justice in French grammar, the first person future would be *allerai*. But no, it is *irai*. Logic, consistency, and justice are as foreign to this grammar as they are to the political institutions in the so-called Republic of Quebec. Take the verb *croire*. Here we have to—"

As Margaret read on, Mona looked at Paul and made a small grimace. He returned the signal, indicating that he too was becoming impatient with the way this meeting was going. Margaret's article was turning out to be just as boring as Robert's.

At the beginning of the meeting there had been excitement in the air, for Guido had told them that tonight the mysterious Kevin would be making an appearance, and some of the details of Operation Thunderbolt would be revealed. Mona had been told that she would be working very closely with Kevin, and tonight she would be meeting him for the first time. She wondered what he would be like.

But two hours had gone by and Kevin had still not appeared. And now Margaret, the tough, wiry-looking guerrilla, was mounting what seemed to Mona to be a totally irrelevant attack on French grammar.

"...reaches its utmost oppressiveness in *venir*," Margaret was saying. "Take, for instance, the past historic tense of this wretched verb. The third person singular is, of course, *vint*. The very same word also serves as the third person singular of the imperfect subjunctive, but here we must place a circumflex above the *i*.

"This completely arbitrary circumflex symbolizes the heavy authoritarianism of the French language and the French philosophy. In English, the speaker is free to utter his vowels at whatever pitch and in whatever tone he wishes, but in French everyone must slavishly follow the command of *dirigisme*. The circumflex hangs over the *i*—the individual—like a heavy black umbrella, shutting out the sunshine of liberty.

151

"The circumflex, the cedilla, the grave accent, and the acute accent – these diacritical marks are symptoms of a yearning for regimentation, of a willingness to surrender freedom in the name of the 'collectivity.' And, as we know, in Quebec this collectivity means the despotism of President Chartrand and the oppression of the Anglos.

"Our revolution will change all that. We Anglos will throw off the yoke of circumflex and cedilla, and we will live in a separate country of our own, an independent country where men and women will be free to put whatever stress they please on their vowels, the noble vowels of Shakespeare, bequeathed to us by ancestors who wrote the Magna Carta and the Bill of Rights."

There was a smattering of applause as Margaret sat down. She looked around expectantly, for comment. Guido was the first to speak.

"If you don't mind my saying so," he said, "that was a complete waste of time. As far as *The Liberator* is concerned, it's useless."

"Oh?" said Margaret. "I – I put a lot of work into it."

"For God's sake, Margaret, what we need is a call to arms, not a grammar lesson."

"You missed the symbolism, Guido."

"We need articles in the paper that'll make people's blood boil. Who's going to risk their life to get rid of a few punctuation marks?"

"You've missed the whole point. It's accents, not punctuation."

"Quiet," Chucky said. "There's somebody out there."

They all listened and heard two sharp raps on the door, followed by a short silence and then a third rap. Chucky got up and unbolted the door. Kevin came in.

"Kevin," Chucky said, "I want you to meet our two new members, Mona and Paul."

"Hi," said Kevin, shaking hands with Paul and then Mona. He had a very firm, positive handshake, Mona thought, and

152

it seemed to her that he held onto her hand for a second or two longer than was absolutely necessary.

"All right," Guido said. "Now we can get on with the main business of the meeting, which is our various assignments for Operation Thunderbolt. I can now reveal that this operation will involve kidnapping – the kidnapping of a very important person.

"Our ransom demands will consist of four items: first, the Anglo Liberation Army's Manifesto must be read on radio and television, and it must be printed in all Quebec newspapers; second, our sixteen A.L.A. comrades who are political prisoners on Nuns' Island must be released; third, the government must provide a plane to fly these sixteen to London; fourth, the government must give us three million dollars in American funds to take to London.

"That money will be used to set up an overseas office of the A.L.A. Kevin and Robert will be going over on the ransom plane, to work in that office. Are there any questions?"

"Who is it that we're going to kidnap?" Paul asked.

"There's no need for all of us to know that right now," Guido said. "You'll learn in due time."

As Guido spoke, Mona glanced at Kevin. He was one of the handsomest men she had ever met, with steady blue eyes and a great mass of blond hair. He seemed at once muscular and graceful, and there was something reckless about the way he sprawled in his chair.

"Has Mona been told what her job is going to be?" Kevin asked.

"I was just coming to that," Guido said. "The man we're going to kidnap, Mona, has a great weakness for attractive women. Kevin is going to arrange for you to meet this gentleman, who will surely try to seduce you. And you're going to lead him on – right into our trap."

* * *

Le Manoir Malbec was on Durocher Street, near the former

153

McGill University. It was an old apartment building that had not enjoyed any significant repairs since Separation. The walls of the corridors were scarred and pitted, and there were ominous stains in the plaster of the ceilings. In most cities of the western world, the Malbec would be classified as third-rate or worse; but in Montreal, as in Poznan or Pyongyang, dwellings like this were considered luxurious.

As she entered the imitation-marble lobby, Mona marvelled at the thought that someone she knew actually occupied an apartment here. It was unheard of for Anglos to live in such splendour, but this Kevin was a government chauffeur, so obviously he could afford it. She glanced at the names on the mailboxes and noticed that Kevin's was the only one that wasn't French.

The elevator had given up the ghost long ago, so Mona climbed the stairs to the third floor. As she knocked on the door of Apartment 31, she hoped her nervousness would not show. But her heart seemed to have been beating at twice its normal rate, for the past half hour, ever since Kevin phoned her and asked her to come over. The kidnapping was still a week away, but perhaps this unexpected summons meant that it was going to happen sooner. She dreaded the prospect of what she was going to have to do, once the operation got started, but she was determined to go through with it.

"Hi," Kevin said. "Come on in."

He closed the door behind her and showed her into the living-room.

"Is there anything wrong?" Mona asked. "Is there some emergency?"

"No, just a few details I've been thinking about," Kevin said. "A few things we ought to work out, so everything'll go smoothly."

He gestured to the chesterfield and she sat down.

"Can I get you a drink?" he asked.

"You mean alcohol?"

"Yes, I've got Québérac, rye, and *whiskey blanc*."

"Oh, uh, well, something very mild, please." It was, she realized, a clumsy and inadequate answer, but she had only tasted alcohol twice before in her life and she wasn't sure what kind it had been.

"How about a Québérac?" Kevin asked.

"Yes, that sounds just right," Mona said, totally ill at ease. This man obviously moved in sophisticated circles that were far removed from the boarding houses of Point St. Charles; in his eyes, she must look like an impossibly awkward country bumpkin.

"This is a beautiful apartment," she said, as he handed her the drink.

"Yes, I guess it is. Would you like to have a look around?"

Carrying her drink, she followed him into the kitchen, where she showed great interest in the greasy old stove and the ancient refrigerator. Then they looked at the bathroom and the bedroom.

"It's really huge," she said, as they went back to the living-room. "How many roommates have you got?"

"I haven't got any. It's just me."

"Just *you*? You mean you don't share?"

"No, only me."

"You mean you have that bathroom all to yourself?"

"That's right."

"It must be terribly expensive."

"It is, but I guess I make a pretty good salary."

"You mean you can make *that* much? As an Anglo without a certificate?"

"Well, it so happens that I do have a certificate."

"You've got a *certificate*? You mean you passed the exam?"

"No, I never took the exam. But I did a few favours for a cabinet minister."

"Oh, I see." She sipped her drink, wondering what he could possibly have done to have gotten himself one of those priceless pieces of paper.

"I don't want to be personal," Kevin said, "but one of the

things I wanted to talk to you about was your clothes."

"My clothes?"

"Yes. I noticed what you were wearing at the meeting, and I see what you're wearing now, and that kind of dress isn't quite right for the kidnapping."

"What's wrong with it?" She suddenly felt indignant. She made all her own clothes and she was reasonably proud of her work.

"It's too – too *Anglo*," Kevin said. "If you don't mind my saying so, it's dowdy. It's too plain, too honest."

"You'd like me to wear something *dis* honest?"

"Look, don't get mad. It's just that for our purposes you ought to wear something with a bit more zing to it. Sexier. Like the French girls wear."

Thinking it over, she realized he was being quite reasonable. After all, her role was to be that of seductress.

"I think I know what you mean," she said. "I can make myself something like that."

"Good. And make it as tight as possible around the behind, will you?"

She felt a surge of embarrassment and indignation. How could he talk like that? How dare he be so familiar? But perhaps he wasn't being personal at all. Perhaps these details were essential to the success of Operation Thunderbolt.

"Can you tell me who it is we're going to kidnap?" she asked.

"I could, but it's better if I don't," he said. "You'll learn a few days before. In the meantime, if you're arrested and interrogated, we'd be able to substitute another girl and carry on with the plan."

"O.K. I suppose you're right."

"One more thing about the way you dress," Kevin said. "When you meet him, come as you are now as far as the top is concerned, if you know what I mean."

"I'm not sure I do know what you mean."

"Don't wear a bra."

"Oh, I see."

"I'll probably introduce you to him at a discotheque. He'll ask you to dance. You've got a great figure and it'll do our friend good to see a bit of bounce on the dance floor."

She felt the blood rise to her face and she wondered whether she was blushing visibly.

"You mentioned a discotheque," she said. "I've never been to a discotheque. I'm not sure I'll know what to do."

"You've never been to a discotheque?" he said, incredulously.

"No, I haven't. Anglos can't afford it. I understand drinks are three or four piastres each. You've probably forgotten just how little an Anglo earns – an Anglo without a certificate, I mean."

"You've got a point," he said. "Come to think of it, I never do see Anglos at discotheques."

"Also, you mentioned dancing. I've never danced. I don't know how."

"You don't *dance*?" Again he was incredulous.

"You've been living like the French for too long," she said. "There's a lot about Anglos that you've forgotten. Of course we don't dance. Where are we going to dance, in the streets? In church? And when are we happy enough to dance?"

"I'm sorry," he said. "But I'm glad we found out in time. I'm going to have to teach you."

He went to the stereo, selected a record, and put it on. "This is the latest dance," he said. "It's called La Choucroute."

He took her by the hand and led her to the middle of the living-room. Then he demonstrated the frenzied gyrations of this newest discotheque mania. He showed her how one shrugged one's shoulders wildly, as though throwing a fit, and how one flapped one's hands above one's head, as though trying to detach them from the arms. Mona was reluctant to try it, but he insisted, and they danced together, flapping at each other like two demented marionettes.

As he corrected her mistakes, Kevin clowned extravagantly,

and soon they were both laughing wildly as they hopped up and down to the throbbing music. And suddenly Mona felt elated. Up till now, ever since she had learned what her role would be in the kidnapping, she had felt revulsion for the whole scheme. But now her disgust was giving way to a kind of excitement she had never experienced before; this was going to be a great adventure – all the more exciting because of the involvement of this man called Kevin.

After twenty minutes of instruction they decided that she had mastered La Choucroute. "You're terrific," Kevin said. "Who says we Anglos ain't got rhythm?"

He poured another drink into her glass and put another record on the stereo. This new music was slow and syrupy.

"I don't suppose you know how to dance La Terrebonne, either," he said.

"No, I don't."

"It's the new slow dance," he said. "You'll have to know that one too."

He took her to the middle of the floor again, but this time, instead of being detached from her, and dancing three feet away, he drew her into his arms and held her closely as he guided her around the floor. At first she was alarmed, feeling that he was making advances, but then she remembered she had seen people dancing like this on television; that must mean it was perfectly acceptable for virtual strangers to press their bodies together so intimately.

"You're catching on very nicely," he said, whispering in her ear.

"Thanks," she said.

The music came to an end, but instead of releasing her he stood with his arms around her. She looked up at him and saw that he was smiling at her. He moved his head slowly down to kiss her, and she averted her lips just in time.

"No," she said. "Please don't."

"You're so lovely," he said. "So exciting."

She squirmed out of his arms and retreated across the floor.

"Well," she said, "I seem to have learned to dance."

"You've done splendidly."

"So now I know how to behave in a discotheque, and I'm going to make myself a new dress, the kind you suggest. Is there anything else?"

"Yes, let's dance some more." He approached her again, and tried to put his arms around her.

"No, Kevin, please," she said. "Let's stick to business."

"Why do we have to do that?"

"Because – because I hardly know you."

"Are we going to get to know each other better?"

"I – I don't know. But not just now. I really have to go." She was at the door and he opened it for her.

"I look forward to our next lesson," he said.

"Yes. Goodbye. And thanks."

As she went down the stairs, she felt strangely exhilarated. But at the same time she felt guilty. It was as though Paul – good, steady, solemn Paul – had been looking over her shoulder, all through that last dance.

* * *

As they walked up Rue Antonio Barrette, Paul kept glancing at Mona. There seemed to be some subtle change in her, and it made him uneasy. Perhaps it was the dress she was wearing; it was quite different from the sort of thing she usually wore.

"That's a new dress, isn't it?" he said.

"Yes, I just made it."

"It's kind of like the French girls wear, isn't it?"

"Yes. Don't you like it?"

"Oh, it's great. But I didn't think *you* liked that sort of thing."

"Well, I do, from now on," Mona said. "I don't see why Anglos always have to look as though they're going to a funeral. Besides, Kevin told me I'd need something like this for the kidnapping. Something sexy."

So it was Kevin's doing. That, Paul realized, was the thing

that was making him most uneasy. He knew she had been up to Kevin's apartment, to discuss strategy, and the thought of the two of them alone there was extremely disturbing.

"You never told me what you discussed, when you visited Kevin," he said.

"Well, we discussed what I should wear for the big event, and then he taught me how to dance."

"To *dance*?"

"Yes. It seems that I may meet the kidnappee in a disco-theque, and he may want to dance with me."

As they walked on in silence, Paul visualized her dancing cheek-to-cheek with Kevin in the dimly-lit, luxurious apartment. The thought was agonizing. Could the dancing lead to something even worse? Or had it already done that? He looked searchingly at Mona, but could find no clue in her face.

When they reached the meeting place, all the other members of the cell were already there, including Kevin. Paul noticed how Kevin directed a broad smile towards Mona.

"I can now tell you more details about Operation Thunder-bolt," Guido said to the members. "The man we're going to kidnap is arriving in Montreal tomorrow. His name is Abakar Ndougou. He's the Foreign Minister of Senegal, coming here to represent his country in the twentieth anniversary celebrations.

"As you all know, Quebec is very anxious to maintain good relations with the French-speaking countries of Africa, and Senegal is one of the most important of those countries. Thus I don't see how our good friend President Chartrand can avoid paying us the ransom that we're going to ask for. It's going to be very, very important for Quebec that this distinguished statesman is released unharmed. One more thing: this whole scheme was Kevin's idea, so we owe him a special vote of thanks. Any questions?"

"Yes," said Paul. "I just don't understand how Mona is going to get to meet the Foreign Minister of Senegal."

"Don't worry about it," said Kevin. "That's all being looked after."

15

The plane bringing Abakar Ndougou to Montreal was two hours late, the Foreign Minister having requested an unscheduled stop in Havana to pick up cigars. At Mirabel Airport, Kevin O'Donnell paced up and down impatiently. Then he sat down and took the fateful letter from his pocket, to reread it for the umpteenth time. It was brief and admirably to the point:

Dakar, Senegal,
April 15

My Dear Kevin,

I am pleased to inform you that I will be in Montreal from June 22 to June 26, to participate in your twentieth anniversary celebrations. I have asked our Embassy to arrange that you be assigned as my chauffeur for that period. As you know, I am interested in meeting stimulating people. I know you will arrange everything and everyone will be very happy.

Please be assured, my dear friend, of my most respectful sentiments.

Abakar Ndougou

Kevin had chauffeured the Foreign Minister on his last visit to Montreal, seven months ago. On their way to the airport, at the end of the visit, Ndougou had said, "You know, my friend, I have enjoyed the embraces of beautiful young women in sixty-three different countries of the world, but my notebook tells me that I have never been with one from your Quebec Anglo minority."

"That's very unfortunate, Your Excellency," Kevin said.

"I understand some of them are extremely desirable."

"That's true, sir."

"If I wanted to meet an enchanting young Anglo girl on my next visit to Montreal, could you yourself, by chance, be able to arrange it?"

"Yes, I think I could, sir."

"I will count on you, Kevin. And this will help you cover any expenses." The Foreign Minister leaned forward in the back seat of the electrocar and handed Kevin a substantial sum of money, in French francs.

Kevin had forgotten all about it, until this letter came. For the Anglo Liberation Army it was a godsend.

Kevin glanced at his watch. Ndougou should be here any minute. He walked across the airport lounge and looked out onto the tarmac, where a brisk tune was being played by the band of one of Quebec's crack regiments, the Voltigeurs de Chicoutimi. The band was greeting the president of El Salvador, who had just arrived for the twentieth anniversary with a large delegation. As the Salvadoreans were whisked through customs, the bandmaster scurried through the ranks of the Voltigeurs, checking their sheet music for the next arrival. With dozens of national anthems to be played at the airport during the next few days, it was all too easy to make a mistake. And the wrong anthem for the wrong dignitary could lead to serious trouble, at a very high level.

As the band struck up what it hoped was the national hymn of Senegal, Kevin went out onto the tarmac. The door of the Air Senegal plane opened and Abakar Ndougou came down the steps. His entourage of twenty people followed, including the Minister of Finance and Ndougou's Parisian chef. In Montreal there was always bitterness in the kitchens of the Ritz when this chef was installed, but Ndougou insisted that few of the world's hotels could meet the standards of his palate.

Alcide Tardif, the Foreign Minister of Quebec, stepped forward and greeted Ndougou. Then, together, they inspected the honour guard, supplied by the Bombardiers de Lachute. Ndougou was a striking figure as he strode past the line of artillerymen. He was a very slender man in his forties, well over six feet tall; he walked with the easy, confident bearing of a member of his tribe's highest caste; his Savile Row suit, immaculately cut, put to shame the tubular garment that Quebec's Foreign Minister had picked up in East Berlin.

As soon as the inspection was over, Ndougou caught sight of Kevin. "*Ah, mon ami anglais!*" he said, going over to shake Kevin's hand.

"*Bonjour, Excellence,*" said Kevin.

"I shall drive to the hotel with my friend Kevin," Ndougou said to Alcide Tardif. "Thank you for your welcome and my compliments to the band. I have seldom heard such a stirring rendition of the national anthem of Mauritania."

As Kevin held the electrocar door open for Ndougou, Tardif watched with displeasure. According to protocol, Ndougou should have ridden with Tardif, who had hoped to use this occasion to try to find out, most casually, what Senegal's latest thinking was with regard to Quebec's application for a loan of 500,000,000 piastres.

"They are irritated that I drive with you," Ndougou said, with relish, as he and Kevin drove off in the blue electrocar. "I told them that I want to practise my English with you, but they cannot comprehend that. It is as though I wished to spend a vacation in a leper colony."

"As you know, Excellency, Quebec has a very particular outlook."

"Yes, I know. But I cannot understand why the authorities here do not act in a more civilized way toward their Anglo minority. In my country, we do it much better. My own people – the Wolof – are the majority, but we show every courtesy toward the Fulani, the Serer, the Diola, the Toucouleur, the Mandingo, the Lebou, and the Moors. Why cannot Quebec act similarly? I asked that question of your President Chartrand, during my last visit here."

"May I ask what his answer was, Excellency?"

"He said Senegal has an older, more mellow civilization than Quebec," said Ndougou. "But I think he was flattering me, so he could borrow 500,000,000 piastres from me."

What a splendid chap this Ndougou is, Kevin thought. What a shame to have to kidnap him.

"And now, my dear Kevin," Ndougou said, "tell me what I am very anxious to hear. Have you arranged for me to meet someone interesting?"

"I have indeed, Excellency."

"*Quelle joie*! Tell me about her."

"She is very young, and very bewitching. She has a heavenly body, and sparkling eyes. She is at once very demure and very wild."

"*Quel bonheur*!" Ndougou said, with a small groan of pleasure. "And what is her name?"

"Her name is Millicent Farnsworth, Excellency."

"Kevin, you are magnificent! Have you any idea what a *frisson* I receive when I hear a name like that?"

"I was hoping you would like it, Excellency."

"When I was a student at the Sorbonne, my colleagues and I were always trying to meet English girls with names like Millicent, or Amanda, or Heather."

"I remember you telling me that, Excellency, the last time you were here."

"Girls with names like that have an extraordinary skin, Kevin. It is like peaches swimming in a bowl of cream. It is done by the wetness of their climate, that complexion."

"I am sure Your Excellency will find Millicent Farnsworth's complexion extremely stimulating."

"Kevin, you are truly a good man. I wish all my ambassadors were as perceptive as you are, and as discreet."

You don't know it, Ndougou, Kevin thought, but you're going to help me *become* an ambassador. Our paths will probably cross in Stockholm or Vienna, as I carry the message of the Anglo Liberation Army through Europe – in my Maserati.

"Can I meet Millicent tomorrow night?" Ndougou asked. "Tonight I must dine with your President, but I have kept tomorrow night open for relaxation."

"Tomorrow will be fine, sir," said Kevin.

"*Quel bonheur!*" said Ndougou.

They were now approaching the Ritz, Kevin blowing his electrocar whistle frequently as they sped past the cyclists on the Boulevard du 15 Novembre, formerly Sherbrooke Street.

"You know, Kevin," said Ndougou, "this is still one of the most beautiful streets in North America."

"It certainly is, Excellency."

They drove past Guy Street, heading east, and Ndougou looked out approvingly at the stately Eglise Saint André et Saint Paul, the graceful Musée des Arts Indépendantists, and the stylish Haut-Rinfret's, where the wives of important civil servants bought their clothes. Then, a moment later, they pulled up in front of Montreal's leading hotel, the Ritz-Carbonneau.

The red, green, and yellow flag of Senegal was flying from the marquee of the Ritz, beside the blue-and-white colours of Quebec. As Kevin turned off the battery of his electrocar, the hotel doorman, dressed as an old-time *coureur de bois*, leapt to open the door. Ndougou stepped out onto the red carpet and the hotel manager came forward to greet him.

"Welcome to Montreal, Your Excellency," said the manager. "And welcome to the Ritz-Carbonneau."

"Thank you," said Ndougou. "This is one of my favourite cities."

"You are very kind to say so," said the manager.

"One always amuses oneself very well in Montreal," said Ndougou, with a small smile aimed at Kevin. "But I think this will be one of my most memorable visits."

"Let us hope so, Excellency," said the manager.

* * *

165

That afternoon, Mona, Guido, and Kevin met for a final discussion of strategy. The kidnapping would take place thirty hours from now.

"One more thing," Kevin said, after they had about covered the main points. "I've been thinking about that office we're going to set up in London. We really ought to have a woman there, on the staff. Mona would be perfect. Why doesn't she come over with us, on the ransom plane?"

"That's not a bad idea," said Guido.

"As it is," said Kevin, "it's going to be all men – me, Robert, and those political prisoners from Nuns' Island. We really need at least one woman."

"Yes," said Guido, "she could probably address women's groups, and things like that. Public relations work."

Mona listened to them, astonished. "Wait a minute," she said. "Don't you think you should consult *me*?"

"Wouldn't you like to come to London?" said Kevin.

"I don't know," Mona said. "This is so sudden."

"You could do good work for us there, Mona," said Guido.

"But I can't," said Mona. "I've got my family here, and my job, and everything."

"Well, I won't order you to go," Guido said. "It's quite a step to take, like going into exile. You wouldn't be able to come back to Montreal until we get our independence, which may be many years away."

"Life in London would be a hell of a lot more interesting than life here," Kevin said.

"I know," Mona said. "But this is so – so sudden."

"Think it over," Guido said. "There's still a few days before the plane goes."

Mona's eyes met Kevin's, and he winked at her.

*   *   *

"Swedish fishballs and turnip pancakes," Mrs. MacVicar announced, as her boarders sat down to supper.

166

"God help us," said Bud Sorenson.

"I remember my late wife once made a Swedish meal that was quite delicious," Mr. Brophy said. "That was before the balloon went up, of course, when we lived in Westmount. We were a small group of friends who visited each other once a month for gourmet dinners. We tried to outdo each other in the cooking. We had some fabulous meals."

"That Westmount of yours was the cause of a lot of our troubles, Mr. Brophy," Lionel Greenspoon said. "It was the symbol of Anglo privilege, the home of the arrogant minority. Its very existence was an insult to the French."

"We worked hard for what we had, and I don't think we were arrogant," Mr. Brophy said. "You know, when I think of the old days I always think of Family Day in Westmount Park, with the picnic and the exhibition given by the Fire Department and the children's sports and the Highland dancing and the Twirlerettes. And of course the novelty races for mothers and fathers – myself in the sack race, and not doing too well, but my late wife astonishing everybody by winning the ladies' egg-and-spoon race. We always had a marvellous time. But was that arrogance, Lionel?"

"You were privileged," said Lionel Greenspoon.

"I suppose we *were* privileged, but no more privileged than the well-to-do French of Outremont. You know, another thing I always remember, from the old days, was walking down Grosvenor Avenue on an autumn evening and smelling that woodsmoke from the fireplaces. On a Saturday night there would be cosy little dinner parties in those houses. In our own circle, we had three McGill professors, and the conversation was always lively."

"You put your finger on it," said Greenspoon. "It was cosy. Too cosy."

When they finished supper, Mona took Paul aside. She looked troubled.

"There's something I've got to tell you," she said. "Guido

and Kevin think I ought to go to London, on the ransom plane. To work in the office over there."

Paul had a sick sensation in his stomach, as though someone had hit him.

"Are you going to go?" he asked.

"I don't know," she said.

He gazed at her unhappily and for some time neither of them said anything.

"Look," Paul finally said, "I wasn't going to bring this up right now, I was going to wait until after the kidnapping. But I – I wondered whether we shouldn't get married."

"Oh," she said, "I – I don't know what to say."

"I really love you," he said.

"I'm confused, Paul. I don't know what I want."

"Doesn't that appeal to you? Us being married?"

"I don't know. I'm not sure of *anything*."

"Can we talk about it?"

"Yes, but not now," she said. "I'm really very nervous. By this time tomorrow I'm going to be with that man from Africa, helping to kidnap him. That's kind of awful, isn't it, when you come to think of it?"

"Yes, I guess it is."

He looked at her sadly. He almost wished that Operation Thunderbolt would fail, so that there would be no ransom plane heading for London, and no possibility that Mona would leave him.

* * *

"Will there be fireworks tonight?" asked Abakar Ndougou.

"No, not tonight," said President Chartrand. "They start tomorrow night, at one minute after midnight. They will usher in a great day for Quebec."

"That is when you celebrate your Proclamation of Sovereignty, is it not?" said Ndougou.

"No, that will be on Sunday," said the President. "Before that we must commemorate the Fourth Referendum, the day

168

the population voted to overthrow the colonial power and become independent."

"Why, if I may ask, is it called the *Fourth* Referendum?"

"Unfortunately the first three referendums failed, thanks to the lying propaganda of the media, the stubborn selfishness of the Anglos, and the criminal interference of the Canadian federal government."

"But the Fourth Referendum succeeded?"

"Yes, for that one we developed some very ingenious strategies."

"Then let us drink to the Fourth Referendum," said Ndougou, lifting his aperitif to his lips.

The President and the Foreign Minister of Senegal were on the terrace of the Presidential Mansion, having cocktails before dinner. With them were other foreign dignitaries and Quebec officials of the highest rank. The men were in white tie, the women in evening gowns, and the generals and admirals in full fig, their ponderous sashes encrusted with medals.

"It is my understanding," said President Chartrand, "that my minister of finance will be meeting with your minister of finance tomorrow, to discuss the question of a loan."

"Yes, I believe that is the case," said Ndougou.

"Personally I stay out of these matters," said the President. "I leave everything to my financial wizards."

"That is precisely my own policy," said Ndougou.

"But I must confess to some small curiosity about the outcome," said the President.

"Yes, but we must have patience," said Ndougou. "I believe we shall have the answer soon."

The President and the Foreign Minister, drinks in hand, strolled over to the balustrade to look down at the city. In pre-Separation days, this terrace had been the Westmount Lookout, at the top of Westmount Mountain. Behind it was the Summit Park Bird Sanctuary, and it was on this large and leafy expanse that Henri Chartrand built his Presidential Mansion. It was a massive structure in which the architect had attempted to

169

blend the modern concrete-blockhouse style with the more refined lines of Versailles.

"A beautiful view of the city," said Ndougou.

"Yes," said the President, "and down there a million people will be rejoicing tonight."

Below the terrace, dusk was descending on Montreal. Bright lights appeared in the shop windows, for the rationing of electricity had been suspended in honour of the twentieth anniversary. Patriotic music boomed out of loudspeakers, which seemed to have sprouted everywhere. In Lafontaine Park, and on the slopes of Mount Royal, young people danced on the grass and drank beer and bought slices of hot *tourtière* from gaily-decorated stalls.

"Do you see those big houses on the hill beneath us?" asked the President.

"Yes, they are very impressive," said Ndougou.

"Before independence," said the President, "it was the great Anglo capitalists who lived there, the exploiters of my people. The robber barons, they were called."

"Who lives there now?"

"My loyal lieutenants, whose only wish is to serve Quebec."

The President's major-domo appeared from inside the mansion and tapped a small gong. Then he led the guests in to dinner. For some of the less worldly visitors, like the chairman of the Bulgarian Workers' and Peasants' Institute, this was a uniquely glittering event, something long to be remembered. But for Abakar Ndougou it was just another state banquet. Tomorrow night's intimate dinner, with the bewitching Millicent Farnsworth, would be far more interesting.

* * *

After driving Ndougou back to the Ritz from the banquet, Kevin went home. As he entered his apartment he heard the phone ringing and he leapt to answer it. It was the Minister of Tourism, Fish and Game—Suzanne Levasseur.

"Why don't you come over for a nightcap?" she asked.

He was about to decline, pleading fatigue, when it occurred to him that this would be the last time he could ever make love to the admirable Suzanne. She wouldn't know that, of course, but tomorrow was Kidnap Day – and then Kevin O'Donnell would vanish forever from the Montreal scene.

"I'd love a nightcap," he said. "I'll be right over."

As he changed from his powder-blue chauffeur's uniform into civilian clothes, he wondered what they would all think when they learned that their former bedmate was actually an Anglo terrorist. What would Suzanne think? And Marie-Thérèse? And Odette, Danielle, Nicole, and Monique? Surely they would be startled.

In a way he was sorry to have to say goodbye to them, especially Suzanne, who had made so much possible for him with that magical Certificate of Linguistic Purity. But saying goodbye was not really too difficult, for that ransom plane would be transporting him into a new world of supple British nymphs, and dark, beckoning Italian goddesses. He had seen their pictures in Suzanne's European fashion magazines.

And yet the woman who interested him most, right now, was right here in Montreal – his fellow freedom fighter, Mona. He was intrigued by the way she had rebuffed him. It was quite some time since any woman had said No to him, so definitely, and that made it all the more imperative that he get her into bed.

Taking her along to London was, perhaps, an extreme measure, but with the kidnap so imminent there simply wasn't time to carry out the necessary amatory manoeuvres on this side of the ocean. He was aware that he would be taking coals to Newcastle, but Mona presented a challenge he couldn't ignore.

Whistling cheerfully, Kevin O'Donnell locked his door behind him and set out for Suzanne Levasseur's luxurious apartment, way up on the seventeenth floor of Le Parizeau.

171

16

It was 7:00 P.M. on the day of the kidnapping. Mona's hands were starting to tremble, to the point where she was having difficulty operating her sewing machine.

On this day, the staff of *l'Atelier national du costume* was to have been dismissed at noon, so they could start taking part in the weekend's climactic anniversary celebrations. But things hadn't worked out that way.

At 11:00 that morning, four officers of the Political Police had marched through the sewing-room into the office of Rodrigue Martineau, the director of *l'Atelier*. Twenty minutes later they marched out, taking Martineau with them, in handcuffs. Madame Tousignant, the supervisor of seamstresses, came out of the office behind them and watched as the policemen and their prisoner disappeared down the stairs.

"He is going where he belongs!" Madame Tousignant said, exultantly. "To Nuns' Island."

"What happened?" several of the seamstresses asked.

"It is as I predicted," Madame Tousignant said. "There has been terrible trouble about the trousers for the Founding Fathers, in the Proclamation of Sovereignty pageant. The actors have refused to wear them because the flies are incorrect, because the entry to the zipper is from the left."

"And he was arrested for *that*?"

"It was not an accident. The Political Police, acting on information that I was able to give them, learned that it was sabotage – a deliberate attempt to confuse and demoralize the actors. Our Anglo enemies would like nothing better than for the world's television cameras to show our Founding Fathers looking uneasy. It would be interpreted as meaning that they had doubts about the wisdom of making Quebec independent."

"And Monsieur Martineau did that on purpose?"

"Yes, he and that little strumpet Lisette, who actually made those flies."

"And they will both go to Nuns' Island?"

"Yes, and let us hope it will be for a long time," said Madame Tousignant. "And now everyone can take half an hour for lunch – and then back to work."

"But we're supposed to quit at noon today," said several seamstresses.

"That's cancelled," said Madame Tousignant. "I'm in charge here from now on, and we have a lot of work to do. All those trousers for the Founding Fathers have to be remade."

Now, at 7:00 in the evening, there were still many hours of work ahead for the seamstresses. But it was urgent that Mona get out of here soon, for she had to go home, bathe, change into her sexy new dress, and go off to meet Ndougou at around 9:00.

Mona's instructions from Guido had been to act as normally as possible and keep a low profile in the days and hours leading up to the kidnapping. It was only common sense. But now she would have to do something very out of the ordinary. Her heart beating quickly, she went to Madame Tousignant's office.

"I am sorry, madame," she said, "but I am sick and have to go home."

"Nonsense."

"I am serious, I am really not feeling well."

"You're the fifth girl who has come to me sick in the last hour. You all want to go to the celebrations, to drink beer on Mount Royal and flirt with the boys."

"I feel dizzy, madame, and feel as if I have fever."

"As an Anglo you should consider yourself fortunate to be able to work here. Now go back to your machine. The Founding Fathers are waiting for their trousers."

"I am sorry, but I must leave."

"If you leave, Mademoiselle Rosenstein, you need never come back."

Mona paused for a moment. The woman's threat, she realized, was not a bluff. But unless Mona left now, there would be no kidnapping.

"Very well," she said. "Goodbye, Madame Tousignant." And she left.

It was the end of her career at *l'Atelier*. She would now be free to join her sister Naomi, washing dirty bottles or sorting old rags. Or, what was a much more attractive prospect, she might fly away to London, with Kevin.

* * *

That night in downtown Montreal there seemed to be a policeman everywhere Mona looked. As she walked through the streets on her way to the discotheque, Mona saw policemen on foot, policemen on bicycles, policemen on horseback. One of their big paddy-wagons, drawn by a pair of Clydesdales, rumbled past her on its way along Rue Ste. Catherine.

Huge crowds were starting to assemble for the twentieth anniversary celebrations, to sing and dance in the streets, and to be entertained by strolling musicians, clowns, acrobats, and unicyclists. The police were presumably on hand to maintain order during these festivities, but to Mona it seemed obvious that their real purpose was to hunt down Anglo freedom fighters.

She turned into Rue du Croissant, the lively street where the city's smartest restaurants, bistros and discotheques were to be found. Halfway up the block she came to Le Pistolet, the smartest of all the discotheques. She was glad to see the government electrocar parked at the curb, with Kevin sitting behind the wheel. That meant Ndougou was inside the discotheque, waiting for her. She and Kevin exchanged the briefest of glances.

There was a large line-up of people waiting on the sidewalk to get into Le Pistolet. Mona, as instructed, spoke to the doorman.

"*Monsieur Ndougou m'attend*," she said.

"*Vous êtes Mademoiselle Farnsworth?*" the doorman asked.

"*Oui.*"

"*Suivez-moi, s'il vous plaît.*"

She followed him inside, into a dark room full of people who were dancing La Choucroute, flailing their arms wildly in the air. Coloured lights flickered intermittently through a heavy haze of cigarette smoke. The music was deafening.

The doorman led her to a table at the edge of the dance floor, where a tall, slender man was sitting. This was obviously the Foreign Minister of Senegal. He smiled happily when he saw Mona and stood up to shake her hand. He was saying something, but with the music so loud she could not hear a word of it. But assuming he had given her some greeting, Mona said, "How do you do."

As she sat down, she wondered whether he would notice how ill at ease she was. Perhaps the noise and the smoke would somehow obscure her nervousness. For the hundredth time she asked herself how she could possibly go through with this dreadful assignment.

A waiter came up to the table and said something she could not hear. She presumed he was asking her what she wanted to drink, so she pointed to the glass in front of Ndougou. She would have the same thing. The waiter nodded and went away.

Ndougou gestured to the dance floor and they got up and joined the other dancers. He was remarkably agile as he staggered and jerked in the contortions demanded by La Choucroute. Mona, remembering what Kevin had taught her, found that she too was doing quite well – heaving, lurching and flailing in the accepted manner.

The dance seemed to go on endlessly, and Mona was pleased to find that its frantic agitation was somehow calming to her nerves; her poise seemed to be coming back; she now felt fairly certain that she wouldn't panic during the tricky manoeuvres that lay ahead.

Finally the music came to a crashing finale and then died out. Mona and Ndougou stood with the other dancers, panting. Then, immediately, another number started – a slow one – and, as Ndougou encircled her with his arms, they started shuffling lackadaisically. They had been together for more than ten minutes, Mona realized, and they had barely exchanged a word, but now that the music was fairly quiet, she waited for him to start a conversation. He did so almost immediately.

"We are talented dancers, you and I," he said.

"Yes, we are," she said.

"In fact we make a lovely couple."

"Yes, we do."

"Millicent Farnsworth is a beautiful name. Do you have a middle name?"

"Yes, it's Samantha."

"Samantha," he said. "Also beautiful. Tell me, do you ride horseback? Girls named Samantha frequently ride."

"I'm afraid I don't, Mr. Ndougou. You see, we Anglos had our horses confiscated a long time ago."

"Yes, of course. How unfortunate. By the way, please call me by my first name – Abakar."

The music sighed on, with a moaning female vocalist joining in:

> I'm just a lazy
> Bundle of nerves,
> I need you, baby,
> To get me started,
> And slow me down.

Mona found it strange to hear music with English lyrics, but at Le Pistolet you could dance to the latest American hits, on records smuggled in from Toronto. No other discotheque in Montreal dared play these illegal vocals, but Le Pistolet was a favourite resort for the sons and daughters of high government officials, and this gave it immunity from the Language Police.

176

"I have a suggestion for a beautiful way to spend the remainder of the evening," Ndougou said. "May I tell you what it is?"

"Please do," said Mona.

"We will go to my suite at the Ritz-Carbonneau," said Ndougou, "and there we shall have a small, intimate dinner. Just the two of us."

Kevin had told her to expect this invitation, and they had worked out a response to it.

"I'm afraid that isn't a good idea," Mona said.

"Not a good idea? Why not? I have my personal chef with me. He is preparing a *Cailles en cocotte Saint-Mars* for us. It will be delicious."

"Unfortunately, Abakar, I cannot set foot in the Ritz-Carbonneau."

"Why not? It is an excellent hotel, is it not?"

"Yes, but I cannot be seen there."

"I don't understand, Millicent."

"You see, Abakar, my father was once a very important businessman in Montreal. But, when the State of Emergency was declared, he lost everything – like all Anglos did. He is now an elevator operator at the Ritz. If he saw me there, going up to a man's room, he would probably kill me. And he might also kill you, Abakar."

"Good heavens! Thank you for warning me, Millicent."

"Otherwise I would have loved to have dinner in your suite."

"This is most unfortunate. But you are right, fathers can be very dangerous."

"But I have a suggestion," Mona said. "Why not come to my apartment? I could prepare a small dinner for us there. Perhaps not *Cailles en cocotte*, but some typical Anglo dish."

"Perhaps fish and chips?" Ndougou said.

"Yes, if you like."

"A magnificent idea!" Ndougou said. "My chef has never mastered fish and chips."

They left the discotheque and got into Kevin's electrocar with Kevin, in his livery, behind the wheel. Treating him as a total stranger, Mona gave Kevin the address of his own apartment on Rue Durocher. And they drove off, through the crowds of revellers in the streets.

"Were they large, the stables?" Ndougou asked.

"I beg your pardon?" said Mona.

"Your father's stables, before they were confiscated. Did he have many horses?"

"Oh, yes," said Mona. "A great many."

The electrocar pulled up in front of the apartment building and Kevin got out and came round to open the back door for them.

"When shall I ask the chauffeur to return for me?" Ndougou asked.

"How about tomorrow morning?" Mona said.

"Splendid, splendid!" Ndougou said. "My dear Kevin, will you please come for me at eight in the morning?"

"Yes, Your Excellency," Kevin said. "And do have a pleasant evening." Kevin and Mona exchanged the briefest of glances. And then Ndougou and Mona went into the building and up the stairs to the apartment. Her hands were trembling as she turned the key and opened the door.

"Please come in," she said.

He followed her into the living-room and she turned on the lights.

"Can I offer you a drink?" she asked.

"Yes, that would be delightful," said Ndougou, sitting down on the chesterfield. She poured two glasses of wine and handed him one of them.

"Would you excuse me for a moment?" she said. "I'd like to change into something more comfortable, to wear in the kitchen while I cook. Would you mind? It'll only take a moment."

"Please do," said Ndougou. "But that moment will seem like an eternity."

She went to the door of the bedroom and paused, her hand on the doorknob. "I can't quite decide what to wear," she said. "I have a pink négligé and a black one."

"Please wear the pink one," said Ndougou. "You will look truly beautiful in pink."

"Yes, but the black one is perhaps more stylish. Why don't I show them both to you and then you can help me decide."

"A splendid idea! I have excellent taste in such matters."

"I'm afraid my bedroom is rather untidy."

"That is as it should be," said Ndougou. "A bedroom that is too tidy speaks of a life without passion."

He got up from the chesterfield and crossed the room in four large strides. She opened the bedroom door and he went in. She stood in the doorway behind him and heard him cry out with surprise and then fall to the floor with a thud.

Guido, Chucky, and Paul had jumped on him and now all four of them were thrashing around on the floor, in the darkness. They made remarkably little noise as they struggled; Guido had obviously succeeded in getting the gag into Ndougou's mouth very quickly.

"Put the lights on," Guido said, and Mona pressed the switch near the door. Ndougou was lying on the floor, securely bound, gagged, and blindfolded.

"You are prisoner of the Anglo Liberation Army," Guido said to him. "You are a hostage. As soon as the Government of Quebec yields to our demands, you will be released. We have nothing against you personally, or against your country. We wish to do you no harm. Please nod your head if you understand the situation."

Ndougou jerked his head convulsively.

"Good," said Guido. "Now we must take your ring and your wallet, to prove to the authorities that you are our prisoner."

Chucky reached into the breast pocket of Ndougou's Savile Row suit and took out an expensive-looking wallet. At the same time, Paul removed Ndougou's large diamond ring. Both items were handed to Mona, who put them in an enve-

179

lope, together with the letter to the authorities that set forth the A.L.A.'s ransom demands. The envelope would soon be put into a downtown trash can, and the police would be telephoned to come and pick it up.

Meanwhile, Paul, Chucky, and Guido carried Ndougou from the bedroom into the living-room, where they laid him on the floor.

"I regret that you will be rather uncomfortable until we transport you to the place of custody," Guido said. "But then we will be able to untie you and remove the gag and the blindfold. In the meantime, it would be best if you did not struggle or try to escape. Please nod your head if you understand."

Ndougou again jerked his head up and down. He had been writhing in the bedroom, but now he lay still.

"Thank God he's thin," said Chucky, as they began to roll him up in the rug.

A few minutes later the three guerrillas carried the rolled-up rug down the back stairs of the apartment building, with Mona following them. In the alley, a horse-drawn milk wagon was waiting, and they quickly loaded the rug into it.

"Are we ready to go?" said the milkman.

"All set," said Guido.

"My goodness," said Paul to the milkman, "I didn't know it was going to be *you*."

"Yes, it's me," said Mr. Brophy. "Long live Angloland!"

* * *

As midnight approached, the band of the Francs-Tireurs de Joliette struck up a lively march. Sitting on the floodlit platform, with a hundred dignitaries arrayed in rows behind him, President Chartrand listened impatiently as the Chief Engineer explained to him how the mechanism would work. This loquacious technician, the President reflected, should never have been seated next to the Head of State; he was far too boring, with his immensely detailed dissertation about volts, watts, ohms, and amperes.

180

The platform, bedecked with blue-and-white bunting, stood at the top of Mount Royal, near the spot where the old illuminated Cross used to stand. The last vestiges of the Cross were gone by now, and the huge new aluminum Q – for Quebec – had arisen in its place. Tonight, at one minute after midnight, the President would inaugurate the Q, lighting it up with a dazzling halo that would be visible as far away as northern New York State.

"At first we were thinking of using sodium lighting," the Chief Engineer was saying, "but there were three factors that made us decide against this. First –"

"Enough," said the President. "Enough."

"I beg your pardon, sir?"

"If you don't mind, no more technical details. I would like to meditate for a moment, in silence."

"Very well, sir."

But before he could close his eyes, the President noticed a police electrocycle bouncing along the gravel path that led up to the platform. It came to a stop and a dispatch rider leapt off it and hurried over to the President's military aide-de-camp. He whispered something to him and handed him an envelope. The aide immediately brought the envelope to the President; it was marked URGENT in large red letters; the President opened it and read:

> The Foreign Minister of Senegal, His Excellency Abakar Ndougou, has just been kidnapped by Anglo terrorists. A command post has been set up at Police Headquarters to deal with this emergency. We require the President's instructions at his earliest convenience as to how to deal with the ransom demands.
>
> Urgel Tremblay
Commissioner of Police

With a flourish, the musicians of the Francs-Tireurs brought their march to an end. There was silence on top of Mount Royal. The President was staring into space. The chief engineer

181

leaned over and whispered in his ear. "Excuse me, Mr. President, but it is time to press the button."

Mechanically, the President got to his feet and went to the podium. He embarked on what was to have been a lengthy speech, but after a minute or so he cut it short and wound it up with a few words of perfunctory praise for the architects, engineers, and sociologists who had carried out the project. Then he pressed the golden button. After a moment he heard a great cheer from the crowds on the streets in the city below. The gigantic Q was now throbbing with a brilliant blue-white light.

As the band struck up the national anthem, it occurred to the President that this should be the high point of his eleven years in office. It was one minute after midnight on June 24. It was exactly twenty years since the day of the great referendum that created a sovereign and independent Quebec. But, the President reflected, tonight was not the high point; in view of the message he had just received, it was perhaps the low point.

"Is everything all right, sir?" said his aide-de-camp, standing beside him at the podium.

"Yes, fine."

"The national anthem is over, sir. Perhaps you would like to return to your seat?"

"What? Ah, yes." He went back to his seat and sat down. The fireworks would soon be starting.

If anything happened to Abakar Ndougou, the President realized, there would surely be no loan from Senegal. And that 500,000,000 piastres was desperately needed. Every centime had already been allocated.

If Senegal didn't supply the money, what country would? The list of potential sources had shrivelled to almost nothing. Yet Quebec couldn't function without foreign loans. In the ecology of international finance, some countries were destined to be lenders and some to be borrowers – and Quebec was a borrower. Like a whale swimming through the ocean, continuously sucking in plankton through its great, open mouth, Quebec must continuously ingest foreign capital. The young republic had a simple metabolism, gulping money down into a ravenous craw and pouring hydro power out through the mighty anus of James Bay. But the borrowing could never stop, for more power stations had to be built to sell more power to Russia to earn more money to pay the interest on the ever-growing list of loans. And there had to be a few rubles left over to buy consumer goods for the people of Quebec.

Now, bathed in the light of the great Q, the band of the Francs-Tireurs struck up a popular tune. And Raoul Renaud started singing the lyrics that had just taken him to the top of the hit parade:

> *Quant aux Anglais, on s'en fou,*
> *On a choisi l'achat chez nous ...*

Nothing must happen to Abakar Ndougou, the President reflected. And yet how could Quebec give in to these despicable terrorists, especially now, at the height of the great national celebration? Surrender was out of the question. But enough of this theorizing. He must get down to Police Headquarters immediately, to take charge of the situation.

As the President got to his feet, he heard another great cheer from the crowds in the streets below.

"What is that?" he asked his aide.

"They have just activated the tail of the Q, sir," said the aide. The President looked up and saw that the mechanism was working very smoothly. He recalled the director of the *Bureau du symbolisme national* telling him how it had been programmed to flick up and down three times every two seconds, to symbolize the virility of the young republic.

17

Ndougou's prison was in the basement of a long-abandoned paint factory on the Lachine Canal, in Point St. Charles. It was damp down here and occasionally a rat would scurry out from behind a rusty vat, but the prisoner was well below ground, and if he chose to shout and scream he could do so to his heart's content.

But there was no outcry whatever from the Foreign Minister when Guido carefully peeled the adhesive tape off his mouth. Instead he merely cleared his throat and murmured, "That's much better, thanks."

"We're sorry to cause you this discomfort," Guido said.

"I don't want to be a nuisance," Ndougou said, "but would you happen to have an aspirin? The smell of paint always gives me a headache."

But none of the guerrillas had one. "I'm sorry," said Guido. "We'll get you some in the morning."

"Don't worry about it," said Ndougou. "It's not serious."

"He seems very civilized," Mr. Brophy whispered to Guido. "Perhaps we could untie his arms and legs."

"Just let *me* decide that, will you?" Guido said. "And now, Mr. Brophy, will you please go home? Your milk wagon outside may attract attention."

"Do I *have* to go?"

"Yes."

"All right, then. Good night, everybody."

"Good night, comrade."

184

Mr. Brophy was extremely disappointed. He felt he had made an important contribution to the operation by transporting the prisoner across town. Surely this should entitle him to have a voice in formulating policy from now on. But obviously the General Wolfe Cell considered this kidnapping to be strictly their show and nobody else's. Mr. Brophy would complain about this at the next meeting of his own outfit, the Lord Durham Cell.

In the basement the guerrillas waited for Guido to decide on the next move. They had brought their prisoner into the small, bare room where he would be kept. In the dim light, provided by candles, they stared in fascination at the trussed-up Ndougou, who was lying on a cot.

With Guido were Paul, Chucky, Margaret, and Robert, the scholarly guerrilla. Mona and Kevin were outside on guard duty.

"May I ask what your ransom demands are?" Ndougou said. "I presume you have conveyed them to the authorities."

"We have four demands," Guido said. "First, we ask that the Manifesto of the Anglo Liberation Army be read on radio and television, and that it be printed in all Quebec newspapers. Second, we ask for the release of sixteen political prisoners, all members of the A.L.A. Third, we ask for an aircraft to fly the prisoners to London. Fourth, we ask for three million American dollars, to be spent on furthering our cause."

"That all sounds very reasonable," Ndougou said. "And I presume you have informed the authorities that if they do not yield to your demands you will terminate my life?"

"That is correct, sir," said Guido. "I'm sorry it has to be that way."

"Nothing to be sorry about," said Ndougou. "You are merely following the standard procedure for this sort of thing."

The guerrillas looked at each other, puzzled. The prisoner was being so incredibly civil. Could it be some kind of trick? If they untied him, would he turn savage and try to fight his way out? But that was most unlikely. After all, there were five

185

people here, in this little room, to restrain him.

"We have a request to make of you, Mr. Ndougou," said Guido. "We would like you to write a note to the Quebec authorities saying that you are being well treated and urging them to meet our demands."

"I will be glad to do that," said Ndougou. "But I cannot write, can I, with my hands tied together and my eyes blindfolded?"

"If we untie you, do you promise not to struggle?"

"I promise."

They untied him and took off his blindfold. He sat up on the cot, stretching his arms and blinking his eyes. He stared at the sub-machinegun that Paul was holding and Paul stepped back into the shadows with it. It was unlikely, though possible, that Ndougou would notice something wrong with the gun; it was magnificently made, in every detail, but it was still carved out of wood. The A.L.A. wouldn't have any real machineguns until they got that three million dollars.

"You would like me to write a note?" said Ndougou.

"Yes, if you would sit over here, please," said Guido. He led Ndougou to a small table, where there was paper and a ball-point pen.

"What is your deadline for them to meet your demands?" asked Ndougou.

"Eight o'clock Monday morning," said Guido.

"Monday morning," said Ndougou, glancing at his watch. "That is about fifty hours from now. A long time. You have been too generous with them." And he picked up his pen and wrote:

Dear Mr. President,

First let me take this opportunity to thank you for the dinner you tendered at your Mansion last night. I shall long remember the historic Quebec dishes you served, never before having partaken of moose meat.

With regard to the present kidnapping, you will be glad to

know that I am in good health and am being well treated. But I wish to make it perfectly clear that unless I am released unharmed you will not receive one centime of that 500,000,000 piastres that your government is seeking to borrow from mine.

I must advise you that the only way to secure my release is to comply with the demands of the Anglo Liberation Army in every particular. I do not think your police will be able to find my place of captivity. But even if they did, and attempted a rescue, I am sure that I would lose my life in the process, as my captors are very desperate men.

In the meantime, please accept my apologies for being unable to join you and your esteemed countrymen for the remainder of your twentieth anniversary celebrations.

Please be assured, Mr. President, of my most distinguished sentiments.

Abakar Ndougou

"That's a splendid letter, Your Excellency," said Guido. "Thank you very much indeed."

"Oddly enough, I may eventually owe *you* some thanks," said Ndougou.

"Oh?"

"I am not entirely unhappy about being kidnapped," said Ndougou. "You see, this ordeal I am now undergoing will win me a lot of sympathy in my country. And there are elections coming up in September. Actually, my prospects for re-election have not been too good, up to now. The press has been making a lot of trouble for me, claiming that I travel in too great a style and do not need to have a private chef with me at all times. Also, there are some scandals involving women. But the drama of my being kidnapped will surely help the voters forget these trifles."

"Glad to be able to help you, sir," said Chucky.

"But there is one special favour I would like to ask," said Ndougou.

"What is that?" asked Guido.

"I presume," said Ndougou, "that during the next fifty hours you will be issuing the usual guerrilla communiqués, threats, etcetera. Am I correct?"

"Yes, we will do that."

"Would you mind mentioning, in these communiqués, that I fought savagely when you first took me prisoner? That I am continuing to resist, throughout my captivity? That you cannot accept responsibility for my fate, because of my ferocity?"

"We will do that, Your Excellency," said Guido.

"We will say that you fight like a tiger," said Chucky.

"Please, not like a tiger," said Ndougou. "The tiger is unknown in West Africa. Better say like a lion. In my country, the lion is highly respected."

* * *

For an hour a steady stream of policemen had been hurrying into Police Headquarters. But now, as the first hint of dawn could be seen in the sky, hordes of them were arriving, jumping off their bicycles and rushing inside. Each man had been awakened by telephone and had been told to come immediately, on the double. Many of them had been on late-night duty, for the anniversary celebrations, and had had only a few hours' sleep. Now, as they sat in the Assembly Hall, waiting for their orders, they rubbed red eyes with their knuckles and tried to suppress yawns.

Upstairs, in the Operations Room, officers darted about answering telephones and moving markers on maps and charts. At the far end of the room, in the glassed-in Command Module, President Chartrand sat with the Minister of the Interior, the Commissioner of Police, and two of the Anti-Terrorist Division's top sociologists. The President was very angry.

"I still cannot understand how this idiotic thing could have happened," he said.

"The Intelligence Branch assured us, Mr. President, that there would be no violence," said the Minister of the Interior.

"Why was the Foreign Minister of Senegal not given a bodyguard?" asked the President. "For God's sake, *why*?"

"We offered him one, Mr. President, but he refused," said the Commissioner of Police.

"You should have insisted," said the President.

"If I may say so, sir, Mr. Ndougou is very active with women," said one of the sociologists. "That kind of diplomat often refuses to have a bodyguard."

"Then he should have been followed," said the President.

"I'm very sorry, sir," said the Commissioner. Like the Minister and the sociologists, he was very nervous. If this thing ended badly, it would surely mean Nuns' Island for the lot of them.

"Would you like a cup of coffee, sir?" asked the Commissioner.

"No," said the President. "I just want you to find Ndougou."

The Operations Room was dominated by a map of Quebec six metres high. It was the Language Police who made most use of it, being able to see on it, at a glance, the ever-changing patterns of cultural crime. A twinkling red light in Ungava, in the far north, indicated that Eskimos had again been caught speaking English at a meeting of their village council; a throbbing blue light near the American border indicated that television sets were being tampered with, so they could pick up re-runs of "I Love Lucy"; an orange light in the Eastern Townships warned that a restaurant was serving English muffins without a permit.

The President, however, was looking not at this map but at another one, on the opposite wall – a huge map of the Island of Montreal.

"With your approval, sir," said the Police Commissioner, "we will immediately start a house-to-house search in every Anglo district. We will start over there, in Verdun."

"You have a remarkable instinct for the obvious," said the President. "I want a house-to-house search *everywhere* in the city, French houses as well as Anglo."

189

"That will take time, sir."

"Just *do* it, will you? Before I become very angry."

"Yes, sir."

"What about publicity, Mr. President?" asked the Minister of the Interior.

"Not a word," said the President. "The police must act discreetly. Needless to say there will be nothing in our own newspapers. But there are many foreign journalists in the city, for the anniversary. They must not suspect that there has been a kidnapping."

"Yes, sir."

"And most important, there must be no shooting. Is that clear?"

"Yes, sir."

"When you find where Ndougou is being kept, I must be informed immediately. We will negotiate and not shoot."

"Yes, sir."

An officer came into the Command Module and handed the Commissioner a slip of paper. The Commissioner read it.

"Aha," he said. "We have just learned, sir, how Mr. Ndougou was actually abducted. It was the work of a government chauffeur named Kevin O'Donnell. The electrocar involved in the kidnapping has been found abandoned and O'Donnell has disappeared."

"O'Donnell?" said the President. "You mean we have *Anglo* chauffeurs in the drivers' pool?"

"He was the only one, sir."

"Idiots!" the President shouted. "Idiots! Idiots!"

* * *

"Up until now I have no complaints about the way you are treating me," said Ndougou. "But this breakfast is an abomination."

"I'm sorry, Excellency," said Paul, "but it's the best we can do."

"Just what *is* this mess you have given me?"

190

"It's called porridge."

"And people *eat* this?"

"Anglos eat it, sir. We don't have much money."

"May I make a suggestion?"

"By all means."

"Take a detachment of your men up to the Ritz-Carbonneau and kidnap my chef. He will cook for us all. We will all benefit."

"I will discuss that with my colleagues, Excellency."

Paul left the room with Ndougou's uneaten porridge. On the bench outside, Chucky and Robert were on guard duty. They were listening to a portable radio.

"Anything on the nine o'clock news?" Paul asked.

"Nothing yet," said Chucky. "But they've only had Ndougou's letter for a few hours. There should be some reaction later this morning."

Paul went down the corridor and into the cavernous main room of the basement. There were cots here, for the guerrillas to sleep on, and they had brought in a small stove and a television set. The room was quite dim, lit only with candles and a few oil lamps.

Paul went to the garbage can with the porridge. As he went, he looked around for Mona. He thought she might be at the stove, but she wasn't. Then he saw her, across the room, sitting on the edge of one of the cots, talking to Kevin. Was Kevin trying to persuade her to go to London? Paul visualized Mona and Kevin walking hand in hand around Piccadilly Circus; he saw them eating together in an intimate little restaurant; he saw them going up a flight of stairs, to a bedroom. He saw it all in hideous detail.

An hour ago, Mona had told Paul that she still hadn't decided whether she would go to London or not. For Paul, waiting for this decision was far more agonizing than waiting to hear whether the government was going to give in and ransom Ndougou.

* * *

191

"What about Costa Rica?" asked the President.

"I'm afraid not, Mr. President," said the Minister of Finance.

"Why not? We've never borrowed from Costa Rica, have we?"

"No, we haven't."

"They have money, have they not? Senegal is not the only country with money to lend, is it?"

"Senegal is not afraid of the United States, sir," said the Foreign Minister. "Costa Rica is."

"It's those Canadian senators in the American Congress," said the Minister of Finance. "They will do anything they can to prevent Quebec from getting the money it needs. They are determined to starve us out."

"I suppose you're right," said the President. "What about Guatemala?"

"Same problem as Costa Rica, sir."

"If I may venture an opinion, sir," said the Foreign Minister, "I think we might be wise to negotiate with the kidnappers. It is essential that we have that loan from Senegal."

"No," said the President. "Quebec will not be humbled by common criminals."

"Damn those Canadian senators!" said the Minister of the Interior.

"*Sales chiens!*" said the Commissioner of Police.

"To think that we offered those Canadians our friendship on the very day that we proclaimed our independence," said the Minister of Culture. "It's strange to remember the phrase: 'sovereignty with association.' If anything, we were too generous with our offer of association."

"It's hard to understand the Canadian mentality," said the President. "One would think that after twenty years they would be prepared to forgive and forget."

* * *

For economic reasons, television in Quebec was limited to four

192

hours daily, in the evening. But for the climactic weekend of the twentieth anniversary celebrations, it was on the air for a full twelve hours each day. And in the basement of the abandoned paint factory, the guerrillas were enjoying the unfamiliar spectacle of T.V. at 2:00 in the afternoon.

They were watching live coverage of the proceedings in the Olympic Stadium, where a huge pageant was being staged to commemorate the fateful Fourth Referendum. As the actors, singers, and dancers went through their complex routines, Mona noticed many costumes she had sewn at *l'Atelier*. But it wasn't this she was watching for; like her fellow freedom fighters, she was hoping that the program would soon be interrupted by an announcement about the kidnapping, and the reading of the Anglo Liberation Army's Manifesto – the first of the kidnappers' four demands.

On the television screen now the actual ballotting in that momentous referendum of twenty years ago was being allegorized. Sinister figures, in black capes and slouch hats, were prancing about with big placards bearing the word NON. Other negative voters carried a banner that said *J'AI OUBLIÉ*. These forces of darkness dominated the Olympic turf, and the orchestra backed them up with scraping, whining, discordant music. But gradually the forces of enlightenment seeped out onto the field, in the persons of beautiful young girls in abbreviated white togas. Mona remembered the instructions for making these togas: they were to be "revealing but chaste."

The girls in white carried placards with the word OUI on them, and some had a larger banner saying *JE ME SOUVIENS*. There were soon hundreds of these "Yes" voters on the field and, with much elaborate choreography, they finally defeated the sullen, black nay-sayers. As the last of these fled the field, trailing their tattered *J'AI OUBLIÉ* banner, the orchestra obliged with a mocking parody of "God Save the Queen." The audience loved it and roared its approval.

"That's the day they killed Canada," said Chucky. "Twenty years ago today."

"Canada deserved to be killed," said Guido.

"Why do you say that?"

"Because it wasn't a nation," said Guido. "We didn't have any national feeling. We couldn't have staged a pageant like that, stupid as it was. We didn't have any symbols."

"But that was the whole beauty of Canada," said Robert, the scholarly guerrilla. "Can't you see that? We were alone among the countries of the world in not being nationalistic. All nationalism is cruel, ugly, and hostile. But Canada didn't have that. It was ahead of its time. If there is ever to be One World, with universal peace, it will have to be like Canada was – unnationalistic. That's why Canada deserved to survive."

"Balls," said Guido. "That's why it deserved to croak."

They kept watching the television screen, but there was still no mention of the kidnapping. Instead the pageant was proceeding with a comic interlude in which several dejected black figures, still carrying their "No" placards, were being marched back onto the field as captives, to be sprayed with white paint. The audience laughed heartily and applauded.

Just then Margaret came down the stairs into the basement. She had been out on her bicycle making a reconnaissance.

"The police are all over town," she said. "They're going from one house to another."

"What about factories?" asked Guido.

"They don't seem to have thought about that," said Margaret.

"Not *yet*," said Guido.

*   *   *

In the Presidential Mansion, the President and his lieutenants were in the Map Room. The President was looking at Asia.

"How about Nepal?" he asked.

"Nepal is one of the irresponsible countries," said the Minister of Finance. "They have money but they refuse to lend."

"How about Burma?"

194

"Burma is another story. They are not solvent."

"*Calice*!" said the President.

*   *   *

"Anything on the radio?" Chucky asked.

"Nothing yet," said Paul.

"That's always been our biggest problem – getting publicity," Guido said. "Back in the 1960s, when the *French* Separatists were putting bombs in mailboxes, everything they did was reported in great detail, by all the media. But there was a free press then, and that made it so much easier for them."

"Do you think the government is going to try to ignore this kidnapping?" Chucky asked.

"They'd love to, if they could get away with it," said Guido.

"But how about all the foreign press and the foreign television that's here for the anniversary?" Paul asked. "Weren't we counting on getting a lot of coverage from *them*?"

"Yes, but first they've got to hear about it," Chucky said.

"I'm afraid we may have to do the ear thing," Guido said.

"You mean cut it off?" Mona said.

"Not right away," Guido said. "First we *threaten* to cut it off. We tell them they have until a certain time to read our Manifesto on radio and television, as a sign of their good faith. If they don't do it, we send them his ear – as a sign of *our* good faith."

"Who does the actual cutting?" Paul asked nervously.

"We'll cross that bridge when we come to it," said Guido.

*   *   *

"I can only conclude that the police are incompetent," said the President.

"We are following several promising clues, sir," said the Commissioner.

"Why should I believe you?" asked the President.

"Excuse me, sir," said the Minister of the Interior, "but the

195

Ambassador of Senegal is on the phone, reporting that Ndougou did not come back to the Ritz last night. He asks if we have any idea where he might be."

"Tell him our intelligence is that Ndougou is with a woman," said the President. "He will believe that."

"Splendid idea, sir."

"Now what about Indonesia?"

* * *

As Mona hurried along Rue Ste. Catherine, a young man fell into step beside her and tried to take her arm.

"*Veux-tu danser?*" he asked.

"*Non, merci*," she said, and hurried on.

It was the night of the Referendum Day celebration and people were dancing in the streets. Coloured lights had been strung up and groups of strolling musicians mingled with the crowds. There was much drinking of the free beer the government had provided for this special night.

Some youths tried to thrust a bottle into Mona's hand, but she ignored them and hurried on. In the sky the fireworks were starting. Walking as quickly as she could, she turned down a side street and found the trash can she had been looking for. She put the envelope into it and went across the street to a telephone booth. She called the police and told them where to find the latest A.L.A. communiqué.

On her way back to the paint factory, Mona once again tried to decide whether or not to go to London. She wondered what it was that kept her from saying Yes immediately. It was such a marvellous opportunity. There was as much theatre in London as in New York, if not more, and surely there she could become a designer. She could fulfil her ambition and not feel guilty about it, for she would be working for the Anglo cause at the same time.

Leaving Paul would be hard. But his talk of marriage frightened her. She wasn't ready for that yet. If she went to London, *that* problem would, of course, disappear. Yes, she definitely ought to go.

* * *

"Thailand?"

"I'm afraid not, Mr. President."

"Pakistan?"

"Not solvent, sir."

Just then the red telephone rang. The Commissioner of Police answered it and listened intently. Then he hung up.

"There has been another communiqué from the kidnappers, Mr. President," he said.

"What does it say?" asked the President.

"If we do not read their Manifesto on radio tomorrow morning at nine o'clock, and on television at two o'clock in the afternoon, they will cut off one of Ndougou's ears and send it to us."

"*Tabernouche!*" said the Minister of Culture.

"Also," said the Commissioner of Police, "the text of the Manifesto must be printed in all the newspapers."

The President paced slowly up and down in front of the huge world map. From Pakistan to India to Burma to Thailand. Non-lenders, all. From Malaysia to Indonesia to New Guinea to the Solomon Islands. Quebec already owed money to some of these – the President forgot which. From Fiji to Samoa to Tahiti. Ah, Tahiti ... surely it was the most beautiful of all French-speaking territories. He wished he were in Tahiti now. He had been there five years ago and they had given him a magnificent welcome, including a remarkable native feast called a *tamaaraa*. Why couldn't the accursed Anglos of Montreal be as civilized as those Tahitian natives? Why weren't they more grateful for the gift of French culture?

From Tahiti the President went slowly to Chile, and from Chile he went to the window and looked out into the night, at Montreal. The fireworks of Referendum Day were reaching their crescendo.

"All right," the President said, "publish their Manifesto."

197

18

It was June 25, the day when Quebec's Proclamation of Sovereignty was being celebrated. Since 7:00 A.M. radio commentators had been talking about the events scheduled for this day: at Jonquière the world's biggest bonfire would be lit; at St. Hyacinthe acrobats, jugglers, unicyclists, and fire-eaters would perform; at Rivière du Loup there would be a mammoth beer-drinking contest.

Other commentators spoke of the past, of the incredible hardships faced by the early settlers, of the glorious days of 1750, when New France controlled not only the St. Lawrence but also the Great Lakes and the Mississippi, all the way down to the Gulf of Mexico.

Suddenly the commentator was cut off, in mid-sentence, and a new voice came from the radio. *"Nous interrompons ce programme,"* said the voice, *"pour vous faire parvenir un bulletin d'information ..."*

"That's it!" Chucky shouted. "That's it!"

"Quiet," said Guido. "Let's listen."

The other guerrillas in the basement stopped whatever they were doing and came to the radio.

"The Ministry of the Interior," said the commentator, "has announced that His Excellency Abakar Ndougou, Foreign Minister of Senegal, has been kidnapped by a group of criminals calling themselves the Anglo Liberation Army. This scum of the earth has threatened to torture their prisoner mercilessly unless a document they call their Manifesto is read on the radio. For reasons that are purely humanitarian, I will now read this so-called Manifesto:

"'Whereas we the Anglos of Quebec can no longer live in the suffocating ghetto that the French have created for themselves;

"'And whereas we can no longer tolerate our status as second-class citizens;

"'And whereas we can no longer abide the government's interference in every conceivable aspect of our lives;

"'And whereas we can no longer live in a country where human rights are considered privileges, to be granted by the government through the whims of its bureaucrats;

"'And whereas we can no longer tolerate the gradual disappearance of our noble and historic culture;

"'We the Anglos therefore declare our intention of separating our historic territory from Quebec, to form an independent and sovereign Anglo state made up of the western half of the Island of Montreal and a portion of the Eastern Townships, these two areas to be linked together by the Autoroute, which will form a neutral, demilitarized zone.

"'As this will be a *democratic* state, we must secure the endorsement of our plan by a majority of the inhabitants of the abovementioned areas. Therefore a referendum, supervised by the United Nations, will be held prior to Separation, it being understood that the new state will maintain a close economic association with the Republic of Quebec.

"'Following are the rules for the referendum...'"

By now the guerrillas in the basement were dancing about with joy, hugging and kissing each other.

"They're giving in!" Guido shouted. "We've won the first round!"

Mona found herself being kissed by Kevin, who seemed to be trying to make it more than just a celebratory buss. Even though she found it quite exciting, she squirmed out of his arms. What if Paul were to notice? Poor Paul was missing all

199

this, being on guard duty in the corridor outside Ndougou's cell.

"We're going to win!" Chucky was shouting, throwing his arms in the air. "We're going to win!"

"Come to London," Kevin whispered into Mona's ear.

* * *

The news of the kidnapping sent all the foreign journalists, in Montreal for the anniversary, rushing from their hotels to the press headquarters that had been set up for them by the government. Here they struggled to get at the limited number of transatlantic telephones. A shoving match between the correspondent of *Die Welt* and that of *Corrière della Sera* broke into fisticuffs.

Film crews from NBC, CBS, and ABC – the first American television reporters allowed into Quebec in many years – were phoning New York for more personnel, more cameras, more film.

In one of the phone booths, the correspondent of the London *Daily Mirror* had been on the line for almost an hour. Displaying typical Fleet Street enterprise, he had hired two huge bodyguards to stand outside the booth and fend off other reporters who were desperate to talk to their editors.

With his story deadline still hours away, the *Daily Mirror* man was taking his time on the phone. "On the other hand, Bert," he was saying, "you might want to build your second paragraph around this Ndougou's legendary horniness. I have it from several diplomatic sources here that he is one of the great international cocksmen of our time. I think we would be very safe to say that he was probably – repeat *probably* – led into the ambush by the end of his prong. You might even be justified in running a three-column picture of some anonymous Scandinavian bathing beauty. Caption it 'Mystery Woman,' question mark. Make sure she's blonde.

"As I said, you can make that your *second* paragraph, but I still think the lead should be his ferocity in captivity. The terrorist communiqués keep emphasizing that he's struggling like a maniac, which means they may have to cut his throat any minute. I know the African papers are playing that angle very big."

* * *

In the Presidential Mansion, President Chartrand was called to the green telephone. President Boulumé of Senegal was on the line.

"I want my Foreign Minister released immediately," said President Boulumé.

"I understand your concern," said President Chartrand. "But we cannot yield to terrorist blackmail."

"If one single hair on his head is harmed, diplomatic relations between our two countries will cease to exist."

"I will take note of that."

"I imagine you would also be cut off by every other member of the Organization for African Unity."

"I will take note of that."

"Very well, Mr. President. My best wishes on the occasion of your twentieth anniversary."

"Thank you, Mr. President."

"Goodbye."

"Goodbye."

President Chartrand put down the phone and stared into space. Then he picked up his glass and sipped from it. It was his third Scotch before lunch. He never drank this much. He had better take it easy; there were momentous decisions to be made.

What was to be done if weeks passed without the police being able to find Ndougou? That was a distinct possibility. What if Ndougou's ear arrived in the mail? What if his body was thrown out of a milk wagon some morning? What if Quebec could never get any more foreign loans? Perhaps he ought to give in to the terrorists, give them what they wanted. That meant three million dollars to open an office in London from which to slander and vilify Quebec. No, that was out of the question. And yet wouldn't total bankruptcy be even more hu-

201

miliating for the young republic?

For the first time in his political career Henri Chartrand felt trapped in the coils of indecision. Decisiveness had always been his strong suit. When others had dithered, during the Great Riots eleven years ago, he alone was resolute enough to seize power and restore order. And while others hemmed and hawed about the rigours of the proposed Linguistic Purity Laws, he promulgated them without a second thought, as soon as he was in a position to do so. The result was stability and continued hope for the survival of the Québécois culture.

As a young man Henri Chartrand had demonstrated his gift for decisiveness from the very beginning of his career as a school teacher. It was not as a pedagogue that he made his mark but as an officer of the Quebec Teachers' Union. His rise through the ranks of that organization was swift, fuelled by a clear vision of what had to be done.

While others wanted to hold endless debates about policy, and discuss abstractions, Henri Chartrand was interested only in action – the grievance, the demonstration, the strike. Over and over again he told the teachers that they must not squander their best energies in the classroom, but must save them for the only arena that really counted – politics. To win there they would have to purge themselves of that bourgeois sophistry called "keeping an open mind." Teachers could never permit themselves the luxury of trying to see all sides of the question. This could only lead to vacillation, whereas decisiveness was the quality most needed in the leaders of Quebec's youth.

From the presidency of the Teachers' Union it had been an easy leap for Henri Chartrand to the presidency of the Republic. All done through decisiveness. But now, in this idiotic kidnapping, he simply couldn't decide what to do.

* * *

At noon, Margaret came back to the paint factory basement with the newspapers, and once again there was rejoicing.

202

L'Autorité, the official government daily, carried the full French text of the Manifesto on its page three. And it appeared in English on the front page of *The Star-Gazette*, the four-page weekly permitted by the government as a gesture to the "principal minority culture." The Manifesto also appeared in Italian, Greek, Portuguese, Spanish, and Chinese in *Le Devoir*, the weekly that was devoted to "minority cultures in Categories 2 to 6."

Kevin produced a bottle of Québérac and poured drinks. Chucky raised his glass in a toast. "To our future country," he said. "To New Canada."

"Unless we call it Angloland, eh?" said Kevin. "Remember, we haven't decided the name yet."

"Maybe neither of those names is any good," said Robert. "Maybe it should be West Montreal, like West Berlin."

The guerrillas were soon debating this issue, as they did so very often. But Paul took no part in the discussion. He was brooding about Mona and he kept glancing at her, hoping that her face would give him some hint as to what she would eventually decide about going to London. He wondered if she was aware of how unhappy she was making him.

* * *

In Mrs. MacVicar's parlour, the newspapers were spread out and the boarders were reading bits of the Manifesto aloud, euphorically.

"I tell you, Wellington Street is a different place today," said Bud Sorenson. "People are walking with a spring in their step."

"And with their heads held high," said Doreen Brewster.

"I used to think this A.L.A. was just a few crackpots," said Spiro Costakis. "But they must be pretty big to do a thing like this."

"I'm going to join them, if I can make contact with them," said Sorenson.

"Don't worry, you'll make contact with them all right," said Mr. Brophy, with a small smile.

203

"I never knew I could feel so proud to be an Anglo," said Doreen Brewster.

* * *

In the basement of the paint factory, Margaret drew Mona aside.

"I hear you're going to London," Margaret said.

"I haven't quite decided," Mona said. "But I'll probably go."

"I understand it was Kevin's idea."

"Yes, it was."

"How well do you know Kevin?"

"Not very well," said Mona. "I've really only just met him. Why do you ask?"

"You're not involved with him personally?"

"No, of course not."

"I don't want to mix into your affairs," Margaret said, "but I thought you ought to know just what Kevin is."

"What do you mean?"

"He's a Don Juan. One woman after another. Love 'em and leave 'em. He's got many, many notches on his gun – including me."

"I don't see what that has to do with *me*," Mona said, indignantly.

"I just thought you should know, in case going to London is part of something personal between you and him. I can tell you one thing for sure, Mona, in London our dear Kevin is going to be very busy with all those English girls."

"That wouldn't bother me a bit," said Mona. "If I go to London it's strictly to represent the A.L.A. It has nothing to do with Kevin."

Just then Paul came out of Ndougou's cell.

"He's complaining about the food again," Paul said.

"Damn it!" said Guido. "Can't anybody here cook up something decent to eat? It's the least we can do for the poor bugger."

* * *

At the Olympic Stadium the crowds were arriving for the Proclamation of Sovereignty pageant. Under the stands, in the
dressing-room area, the actor who was playing Camille Laurin
stood at a urinal next to the actor playing René Lévesque.
The actor who was playing Jacques Parizeau came in and took
up his position next to him.

"I'm glad they got these damn pants remade," said René
Lévesque.

"Did you hear that it was sabotage?" asked Camille Laurin.

"No, I haven't heard that."

"It was that fellow Martineau, the director of *l'Atelier national du costume*. He and his girlfriend thought they could
demoralize us if they put the zippers in wrong. They're on
Nuns' Island now."

"*French* saboteurs?" said Jacques Parizeau. "I thought only
Anglos were enemies of the state."

"Unfortunately we have plenty of traitors of our own," said
Camille Laurin. "Haven't you ever seen *Québec-Libre*?"

"No, I haven't. What *is* it?"

"It's an underground publication. In French. They claim
they want a return to democracy in Quebec."

"*Bourgeois* democracy?" asked René Lévesque.

"Yes."

"Then they too deserve to be on Nuns' Island, don't they?"
said Jacques Parizeau.

"Of course," said Laurin.

The actors playing Lévesque and Parizeau exchanged a
glance. They were old friends and, like many people in the
theatre, they harboured strong democratic yearnings. But they
couldn't be sure about Laurin, who always talked the straight
government line and might well be a spy. Thus it was a good
idea to deny even knowing of the existence of *Québec-Libre*,
although they were both avid readers of that brave little *samiz-
dat*.

That very morning, before coming to the stadium, they had
both read the special twentieth-anniversary issue of

Québec-Libre. It was full of inspired articles attacking the government and all its works. The actor playing René Lévesque had been particularly interested in an essay that set the record straight about what had really happened in the Battle of Pointe Fortune, twenty years ago. And the actor playing Jacques Parizeau had particularly enjoyed a diatribe aimed at *les Marmots Gatés* – the Spoiled Brats.

These notorious brats were the sons and daughters of high government officials. *Québec-Libre* was exasperated by their costly American-style clothes, their arrogant ten-speed bicycles, and their large expenditures of money at discotheques like Le Pistolet. "These are the privileges of the children of the elite," said the clandestine journal. "Is this what President Chartrand means when he says he has given us 'socialism with a human face?'"

"My zipper still isn't right," the actor playing Camille Laurin was saying. "It only opens halfway down."

"That must make it quite difficult to aim," said Jacques Parizeau.

"I think the sabotage is more widespread than we might suspect," said Laurin.

The three actors zipped up and left the urinals. Upstairs, in the stands, the crowd was waiting for the pageant to begin.

*　*　*

In the Presidential Lounge of the Olympic Stadium, President Chartrand was talking to the Minister of the Interior.

"I am very disappointed in the police," the President said.

"Something has just occurred to me, sir," said the Minister of the Interior. "Now that the public knows that there has been a kidnapping, should we not make some appropriate gesture? Like invoking the Emergency Measures Act?"

"*Niaiseux!*" the President said, in a loud voice. "*Crétin!* Don't you realize that the Emergency Measures Act is *already* in force? I invoked it eleven years ago, at the time of the Great

Riots. It has never been *re*voked."

"Oh, yes, of course," said the Minister of the Interior, nervously. "How silly of me to forget."

"What you will do," said the President, "is declare a state of apprehended insurrection. You will arrest four or five hundred Anglos – it doesn't matter who – and you will put them on Nuns' Island. You will do this with the maximum amount of publicity, so the world will know that we are facing a massive uprising by a traitorous minority, not just another sordid kidnapping by a handful of thugs. This will gain us widespread sympathy, at least throughout the French-speaking world."

"That is a brilliant idea, Mr. President," said the Minister of the Interior.

"Of course it is," said the President. "Now get out of here and get those arrests started."

As the Minister left the lounge, the President again heard the crowds of people in the stadium. They sounded louder now, restless. The pageant should start at any minute. The President waited for his aide-de-camp to come and take him to the Presidential Box.

* * *

The guerrillas watched the pageant on television, and again Mona recognized many costumes she had worked on. She was particularly proud of the ruffled cuffs worn by the Woman of New France. But her fellow freedom fighters seemed distracted.

"We're going to have to send another communiqué," said Guido.

"What will we say this time?" asked Robert.

"We will simply remind them that time is passing and that our deadline is eight o'clock tomorrow morning. If that ransom plane is not ready to take off for London at that time, with the political prisoners and the three million dollars, we will be forced to terminate Ndougou's life."

"Would we really do that?" Paul asked, alarmed.

"Of course not," said Guido. "But we've got to pretend we would."

On the screen, the pageant was entering a comical phase. A phalanx of Allegorical Anglo Capitalists of the Colonial Era was struggling across the field, pushing money bags that were so large and ponderous that they could barely budge them. The crowd roared with laughter, but the laughter died out and was replaced by grim silence as gangs of French Canadians, stripped to the waist and hitched up like Eskimo sled dogs, were made to pull the money bags around the cinder track, whipped on by the fat and slobbering Anglo Capitalists.

"They've certainly got a good script," Kevin said.

Mona found herself looking at Kevin again. There was something cynical about him that was disturbing. He had been telling her how well he planned to live in London and she wondered about his real motive in thinking up this kidnap plot. How much was Anglo patriotism and how much was pure selfishness?

Also, it wasn't hard to believe what Margaret had told her: that Kevin was an inveterate skirt-chaser. But what did that have to do with Mona? Reluctantly she had to admit to herself that it had become a factor in her reckoning. Life in London, with Kevin, might be adventurous, but it was the kind of adventure that might end with her being deserted in a strange country. Like many Montreal Anglos, in this Age of the Bicycle, Mona had never been more than fifty kilometres from home; the thought of being all the way across the ocean, alone and unable to come home, was far too intimidating.

But life with Paul, while not adventurous, would be solid and safe. Yes, perhaps she should decide *against* London.

* * *

In the press box, journalists from many lands were watching the Proclamation of Sovereignty pageant.

"Can you make out what's written on those big bags those

208

chaps are pulling?" asked the *Daily Mirror* correspondent.

"Those are dollar signs," said the man from *Die Welt*. "The dollar was the unit of currency that was used in Canada."

"I find this a bit of a bore, don't you?" said the *Daily Mirror*.

"Quite the contrary," said *Die Welt*. "The symbolism is fascinating."

"By the way," said the *Daily Mirror*, "my editor is after me to check on a rumour that this Ndougou chap goes around the world offering huge sums of money for young virgins. Have you heard anything about that?"

"No, I haven't," said *Die Welt*. "But my editor is now less interested in the actual kidnapping drama than in the political aspects."

"What do you mean, political aspects?"

"Haven't you read the A.L.A. Manifesto?"

"Yes, but that's just typical terrorist stuff, isn't it? Same as the crazies all over the world."

"It is a very serious document. It is a cry from the heart of an oppressed minority. A minority the world has scarcely ever heard about. And yet they number almost a million people. Many of them are being arrested at this very moment."

"A cry from the heart, eh? What's this minority called?"

"They're the Anglos, of course. They are in a state of apprehended insurrection."

"Anglos, eh? I must look into that."

19

The Proclamation of Sovereignty pageant was over. A choir of five hundred voices had chanted the words of the Charter of the Republic while the Founding Fathers, secure in their rectified trousers, had affixed their signatures to a replica of that momentous document.

As the audience left the Olympic Stadium, champagne was served to the President and his guests in the large, glassed-in Presidential Box. The mood was buoyant, with everyone trying to put the kidnapping out of their minds. But the Foreign Minister of Quebec looked solemn as he drew the President aside.

"I have just been talking to the Soviet Ambassador, sir," the Foreign Minister said. "He is very angry."

"Why?"

"You remember the large loan the Russians gave us in February? The Ambassador has just learned that we spent all the money on these anniversary celebrations. He is furious about that. He said the loan was to help us revitalize our industries so we can stand firm against American pressures. It was not for pageants and free beer for the populace."

"Did you tell him that in Quebec we are more interested in the human spirit than in materialism?" the President said. "Did you tell him we would rather build national pride than factories, with all their filthy pollution?"

"I said something to that effect," said the Foreign Minister. "But the Russians don't see it that way."

"Then that's *their* problem," said the President, starting to walk away.

"Excuse me, sir," said the Foreign Minister, detaining him, "but it's *our* problem. The Soviets are calling their loan. They are drawing up a schedule of repayments, to start very soon."

"How can we repay when we are not solvent?"

"The Ambassador says they will accept increased imports of hydroelectric power in lieu of cash."

"But James Bay is already working at full capacity. The Russians already get all the power we can possibly generate."

"Then we must build new power stations."

"How can we do that, when we are not solvent?"

"Don't you see, sir?" said the Foreign Minister. "We *must* have that loan from Senegal. We *must* accommodate the kidnappers."

* * *

"How long is it since they got our last threat?" asked Kevin.

"About two hours, I would say," said Chucky.

"I suddenly feel that maybe they're not going to give in," Robert said, glumly. "Maybe we'll never see New Canada."

"You're right," said Guido. "We'll never see New Canada because it's going to be called Angloland."

"Now wait a minute," said Paul, "that hasn't been decided yet."

"Angloland is the only answer," said Guido.

"Why?" asked Mona.

"New Canada sounds synthetic, plastic," said Guido. "Angloland has some human juices to it. It makes you think of a historic race of people. You think of history's noble Anglos – Dante, Michelangelo, Garibaldi, D'Annunzio."

"Do you realize," said Paul, "that if we call it New Canada it might become the nucleus of a *reconstituted* Canada? How do we know that Ontario and Nova Scotia and all the others aren't tired of being American states? They've never been fully accepted down there. Maybe they'd come together again, up here, in New Canada. A free, democratic, bilingual country."

"*Bilingual?*" said Guido. "Are you out of your cotton-picking mind?"

"Of course, bilingual," said Paul. "There are quite a few French people living in the western half of Montreal, and in the Townships. They'll have their own French schools and everything."

"Over my dead body," said Guido. "If they want to live in Angloland they'll bloody well speak our language – which is English."

* * *

In the great dining hall of the Presidential Mansion, a state dinner was being held for foreign dignitaries. During the first few courses the President, deep in thought, toyed with his food, eating only a few forkfuls. He was usually a good dinner partner, but tonight he had almost nothing to say to the talkative wife of the President of Albania, who sat at his right.

As the waiters started bringing the main course, he made his decision. He got to his feet and with a knife he tapped a crystal goblet. The guests looked up in surprise; the speeches were not scheduled to begin until after dessert. The hum of conversation died down.

"Ladies and gentlemen," said the President, "I have an important announcement. We are all saddened tonight by the absence of His Excellency Abakar Ndougou, who has been kidnapped by criminal elements. While we at this table rejoice in Quebec's historic cuisine, such as *ragoût de boulettes*, our friend Abakar is probably lying in a filthy dungeon, barely subsisting on the unsavoury concoctions that are habitually eaten by our Anglo minority.

"Worse than that, poor Abakar knows that his life may be snuffed out at any moment. Yet despite this, he struggles with the ferocity of a lion. Even his cowardly captors admire this, for they refer to it in all their so-called communiqués.

"When one government gives in to terrorists, all governments ultimately suffer. This has been my only consideration up until now in refusing to deal with the kidnappers of our colleague. But now the instincts of my heart have come to prevail over the colder calculations of my brain. Abakar Ndougou, noble lion that he is, must not die.

"Therefore, on purely humanitarian grounds, my country will accede to the demands of the criminals. Their fellow bandits will be released; they will have their ransom money; they will have their airplane to leave the country. Quebec will be well rid of them. But our colleague, the esteemed Foreign Minister of the great nation of Senegal, will be back in our midst. I thank you."

The applause was loud and long. When it died down, the Ambassador of Uruguay, as dean of the diplomatic corps, got to his feet and thanked the President for his courageous action. There was more applause.

Meanwhile, the President took out his golden pen and wrote a note to the Commissioner of Police. "Make sure," it said, "that the police keep searching until the last possible minute."

* * *

The guerrillas heard the news on the radio. This time there was no dancing in the paint factory basement, no shouts of victory or kissing. It seemed to be a solemn occasion—almost historic—a time for handshakes and quiet congratulation. But the impact was too much for Margaret, and she wept quietly in a corner. And there were tears in the eyes of some of the men too.

The radio announcement included a recording of the President's remarks at the state dinner. Then the announcer said that the Swiss Ambassador had agreed to act as intermediary between the government and the guerrillas; he would be the guarantor of the government's good faith in the delicate manoeuvres that lay ahead. This was another victory for the guerrillas, for it was they who had requested the Swiss Ambassador.

The announcer said that the ransom plane would be ready for take-off at 8:00 A.M.—just nine hours from now. In the meantime, the guerrillas were asked to make telephone contact with the Swiss Ambassador.

But just then Robert came running down the stairs from the ground floor, where he had been on lookout duty.

"The police!" he shouted. "They're coming down the street, checking the factories. They'll be here in a few minutes."

"All right, everybody, let's go!" said Guido.

The guerrillas were well-rehearsed for this emergency. Margaret and Kevin rushed around the big room, putting out candles and oil lamps and pushing the radio and the television set out of sight. Guido, Chucky, and Robert ran into Ndougou's cell, where they quickly bound his hands and feet and put adhesive tape across his mouth, to prevent any outcry.

"Sorry about this, Your Excellency," said Guido, "but the police are on their way. We must be sure you won't make trouble."

Ndougou, attempting a smile through the adhesive tape, nodded his head sympathetically.

Meanwhile, Mona and Paul ran down the corridor to the room the police would enter first, when they came down the stairs. Every effort must be made to head them off here, to keep them from going further into the basement.

"I wish we didn't have to do this," Paul said.

"I know," said Mona. "It's awful."

"Let's hope it works."

Paul quickly lit a candle, to give a glimmer of light in the pitch-black room. Then, as he and Mona heard the police coming into the factory, on the floor above, they tore off all their clothes.

When the first policeman came down the stairs with his flashlight, he saw two young lovers lying on an old mattress on the floor. The lovers sprang to their feet, dismayed, and stood cowering, the girl trying to hide her nakedness with her hands.

"Hé, Pierre, viens voir ça!" the policeman called out, and after a moment his partner, an older man, came down the stairs. He looked startled.

214

"Please give us a break, sir," Paul said, pleadingly. "We're Anglos and we don't have anywhere to go, to be private."

"Have you seen any kidnappers here?" the younger policeman asked, with a wink to his partner.

"What do you mean?" Paul asked, with a puzzled look on his face.

The younger policeman aimed his flashlight directly at Mona, who was standing in the classic pose – left hand in front of the pubic area, right hand and arm trying to conceal the breasts.

"Should we ask her to put her hands up?" the younger policeman said to his partner, grinning. "Maybe she's concealing a weapon."

"Stop that, Gaston," said the older policeman, who seemed embarrassed. "Let's get out of here. We've got work to do."

The two policemen went up the stairs, the younger one pausing at the top for a last look at Mona. And then they were gone.

"Oh, Paul, that was so *awful*!" Mona said.

Paul noticed, for the first time, that she was trembling, and he put his arms around her and drew her close. They stood that way for some time, in the dim candlelight, their bodies pressed together, each savouring the other's nakedness. Then, slowly, Paul started to caress her back and her buttocks. He felt her breathing deepen and they kissed. She reached down and touched his penis.

"It's so hard," she murmured.

They looked into each other's eyes. They had never been more ready to make love – except that the time and the place could not possibly be more inappropriate, what with their fellow freedom fighters just down the corridor, sitting in the dark with their prisoner, waiting for the police to burst in on them at any moment.

"I suppose we ought to let them know the coast is clear," Paul said.

"Do we have to?" Mona murmered, slowly stroking his erection with her fingertips.

"Did I hear you say the coast was clear?" came a whisper from the darkness of the doorway that led back into the basement.

"Oh, Christ!" said Paul. "Is that you, Chucky?"

"Yes, can I come in?"

"No, please don't. We're ... uh ... not decent."

"O.K. But have the cops really gone?"

"Yes."

"Great! I'll go and tell the others."

"Will you do that?"

"Yes. You two just carry on with whatever you were doing."

Paul and Mona looked at each other dejectedly. It was, of course, impossible to carry on—not now. The spell was completely broken; and besides, the whole basement would soon be lit up again, with everybody getting ready for the complex job of exchanging Ndougou for money and an airplane.

They started to get dressed, and as they did so Paul felt suddenly elated. How could he have been so stupid, all these months? *This* was the place to make love—this abandoned paint factory. Or any of the other factories—there were so many of them—that stood deserted in Quebec's Post-Industrial Age. Why hadn't they ever thought of that? As soon as the kidnapping was over, they could come back here and consummate their love. They could come here every night. It would be their nest. But then Paul had a chilling thought.

"What about London?" he asked. "Have you decided if you're going to go?"

She was buttoning up her dress, in the back, and she never looked more beautiful than she did now, in the candlelight.

"Yes, I've decided," she said. "I'm *not* going. My place is here, Paul—with you."

216

20

The correspondent of the *Daily Mirror* was on the phone to his editor in London.

"They're called Anglos," the correspondent said.

"What do you mean by Anglos?" the editor asked. "Anglo-Saxons?"

"I don't think so, Bert, but I'm still checking that. I think they're more like half-breeds. But there's definitely some British blood there."

"And you say they're oppressed?"

"Very oppressed, Bert. They live in filthy hovels and eat bad food."

"I like the sound of this, Fred. I think it'll be front page."

"I just thought you probably had enough of that Ndougou chap. After all, that's just another kidnap. But here we have a peculiar pocket of English-speaking people that nobody ever heard of. Ground into the dust by the French jackboot."

"Can you get me photos of their filthy hovels?"

"I have a photographer on that right now, Bert."

"You say these Anglos are forced to work for starvation wages?"

"That's right. They do all the menial work here."

"Can you get me some undernourished-worker shots, Fred? Some mother-and-child-in-rags shots, with the child's face smudged with dirt?"

"I'll put some of those on the Wirephoto tomorrow, Bert."

"Could we use a headline saying 'Britons Never Shall Be

Slaves' and put a question mark after it?"

"Yes, that would be very appropriate."

"I think we're onto something, Fred. England is going to sit up and take notice."

* * *

"I know it will be uncomfortable for you," Guido said, "but at this point we can't afford to take any chances. So on the way to the airport, your hands will have to be bound behind your back."

"My dear friend, please don't worry about it," said Ndougou. "You are merely following standard procedure for hostage work."

"Also, one of our men will have to hold a gun to your head, all the time. Just to discourage the police from trying any last-minute tricks."

"A very sensible precaution."

"And of course you realize, Mr. Ndougou, that you'll be going along to London with our little group."

"Yes, I took that for granted. If you released me here, or at the airport, the police could assault you immediately afterwards. Or the plane might turn back, after you were aboard."

"Sorry for the inconvenience."

"Not at all. I always sleep well on airplanes. I'll simply take the return flight back to Montreal. I shall have to be here to work out the details of a loan with the Quebec government."

"Is there anything we can do to make things easier for you, Mr. Ndougou?"

"Yes, there is. Would you please make sure that the foreign press get lots of photographs of that gun being held to my head on the way to the airport? I shall want to use that photo on my election posters."

* * *

It was 5:00 A.M. The Swiss Ambassador was coming in an hour in his electrocar to take Ndougou, Kevin, and Robert to the

218

airport. Robert, a skilled writer, would be useful for propaganda work in the London office. Also, Robert would alternate with Kevin in holding the gun to Ndougou's head on the way to the airport.

"Are you *sure* you don't want to come?" Kevin said to Mona.

"Yes, I'm sure," Mona said. "My place is here in Montreal." She looked at Paul as she said it and he smiled happily.

"I wish you could all come with us," Robert said.

"I'd love to see London," Guido said, "but we've got lots of battles to fight here at home. Maybe even with the guns you'll be buying for us."

"Can't we avoid bloodshed?" Mona asked.

"I hope we can," said Guido. "And we will, if the French let us have *our* referendum, the same as they had theirs, twenty years ago."

"By the way," Kevin said casually, "what about that three million American dollars?"

"The Swiss Ambassador will have it in a suitcase," said Paul. "That was just on the radio. Also, the sixteen political prisoners are already at the airport."

"Well, I guess it's time to say goodbye," said Guido. "The rest of us better be gone by the time the Ambassador comes. The police are going to be all over this place, as soon as Ndougou leaves. You go first, Margaret. We'll go one by one, so as not to attract attention."

"Goodbye, Kevin," said Margaret. "Goodbye, Robert." She kissed them both.

"When we meet again, Margaret, it will be in our own country, free and independent," Robert said, a tear in his eye. Margaret wept quietly as she went up the stairs and out of the paint factory, to pedal away into the city.

"You go next, Paul," said Guido. "But wait five minutes, eh?"

"Can I go in and say goodbye to Ndougou?" asked Paul.

"Why not?" said Guido.

Paul pulled on his face mask and went into the cell. Kevin watched him go, fascinated. When Paul came out, Kevin said, "It suddenly occurs to me that Mona is going to *have* to come to London with Robert and me."

"What do you mean?" said Guido.

"I don't know why I never thought of it before," said Kevin. "But when you guys go in to see Ndougou you always put on your face mask first, so he'll never be able to identify you in the future. But he knows exactly what Mona looks like, just as he knows what I look like. He had a very long look at her on Friday night, didn't he, when he thought she was called Millicent Farnsworth?"

Paul and Mona looked at each other, stunned.

"Ndougou wouldn't go after Mona, would he?" said Chucky. "He seems so friendly to us."

"Don't kid yourself," said Kevin. "He's acting friendly now because he figures that's his best strategy as a prisoner. But when he gets back to Montreal, he'll be very happy to help the police track down the kidnappers."

"Kevin's right," said Guido. "And the police will take him right down to the Minority Cultures Registration Centre. He'll go through the registrations of all Anglo girls Mona's age until he comes to Mona's picture. And then it's all over for her. But in London she'll be outside Quebec's jurisdiction."

"Oh, Paul," said Mona, "what should I do?"

But Paul seemed unable to answer.

"I think she has to go to London," Guido said.

"Yes," Paul finally said, "I think she has to go."

Mona and Paul walked down to the far end of the basement and stood in the shadows, out of sight of the others. Paul looked stricken. He put his arms around her.

"How long do you think it will be, before I can come back?" she asked.

"Not until we get our independence," he said.

"When will that be?"

"It's going to be a long time, Mona."

"Will you go and see my parents and tell them what happened?"

"Yes."

They stood in silence. As he clasped her, she was very aware of the hardness of his body, the strength of his arms. In the past, the thought of that had always made her feel protected.

"Hurry up, Paul!" Guido shouted. "You've got to get out of here."

"Goodbye, Mona," Paul said.

"Goodbye, Paul."

* * *

Despite efforts of the government to prevent it, the world's press was out in force at the airport. The journalists were not allowed to interview the sixteen political prisoners from Nuns' Island, but as they boarded the aircraft the prisoners obliged with clenched-fist salutes, and these were very pleasing to the American television cameramen.

The Swiss Ambassador drove Mona, Kevin, Robert, and Ndougou to the airport at top speed, escorted by police electrocycles with their sirens howling. The aircraft that awaited them was not Air Quebec's rickety Ilyushin 371, which they had expected, but a gleaming Air Senegal supersonic jet, especially sent by the President of Senegal. Inside, Mona was astonished by the sumptuousness of the furnishings.

"Perhaps you could sit with me, Millicent?" Ndougou said. "I would like to get to know you better."

"I'm sorry, Your Excellency," Kevin said, "but Millicent and I have some business to discuss. Perhaps she can join you later in the flight."

Kevin gestured for Mona to sit down beside him in one of the luxurious first-class seats. Robert kept his wooden machinegun trained on Ndougou as the plane taxied down the runway and took off. In their seats, the political prisoners squirmed with excitement.

For the first time this morning Ndougou seemed disgruntled.

221

Obviously he felt he had earned the right to sit with Mona. But suddenly his face lit up. Coming down the aisle toward him, from the galley, was a tall man in a white chef's uniform.

"Pierre!" Ndougou said happily.

"Your Excellency, I am so happy to see you safe and sound."

"Pierre, I am almost starved."

"Your troubles are over, Excellency. I am now preparing for you a *Suprêmes de canneton Rouennais*, exactly the way you like it. So I must hurry back to the galley. With this supersonic jet, we will be in London so soon that I hardly have time to make my *Bigarade* sauce."

*   *   *

The London *Daily Mirror* man was on the phone to his editor.

"I tell you, Bert, she's a beauty," he said.

"Are you sure?" asked the editor. "Most of these female freedom fighters aren't much to look at."

"This one is different, Bert. Make sure you have a photographer at the airport when she arrives."

While the man from the *Daily Mirror* spoke on the transatlantic telephone, other correspondents sat at their typewriters composing stories for the *New York Times*, the *St. Louis Post-Dispatch*, the *Neue Zürcher Zeitung* of Zurich, *Le Monde* of Paris, *Die Welt* of Hamburg, *La Stampa* of Turin, the *Asahi Shimbun* of Tokyo, the *South China Morning Post* of Hong Kong, the *Times of India*, and many other influential papers.

The foreign correspondents wrote highly dramatic accounts of the scene at Mirabel Airport, but they reserved their most vivid prose to describe the little-known plight of the Montreal Anglos. Several correspondents called them "the forgotten people."

"But from now on," wrote the man from the *Washington Post*, "we can expect to hear a great deal more about the struggle of these militant Separatists."

222

21

They were Sakurajima radishes, the very large ones. The seeds were to be sown in drills about a foot apart. They would mature in two months.

As Paul stooped over the furrow, he listened to the little transistor radio clipped to his belt. By now the plane should be in London, and he hoped there might be some news of it. But he wasn't surprised when the newscast made no mention at all of the kidnapping and its aftermath. Obviously the authorities were acting as though nothing had happened; the sooner it was all forgotten the better, as far as they were concerned.

Instead of the kidnapping, the commentator spoke mostly about the commemoration of the Battle of Pointe Fortune, which was today's big anniversary event. It was one of the month's twenty-one public holidays for the French, but it was not one of the nine holidays granted to the Anglos. For Paul it was a day when radishes had to be planted.

As he went on sowing his seeds, he thought of Mona. He knew that the ache she had left in his heart would be there for a very long time. He tried to ease the pain by thinking of himself as a soldier, and of her as a soldier too. These were the fortunes of war. He thought of all those young subalterns in the G.A. Henty novels, up in the Khyber Pass or out in the Ashanti jungles. Their arduous duties left no room for women in their lives.

He thought of General James Wolfe. Not much room in his life, either, for women. It was very likely that when Wolfe died at Quebec, on the Plains of Abraham, at the age of thirty-two, he was still a virgin. But around his neck he wore a locket, and inside it there was a tiny portrait of his fiancée, Katherine Lowther. Mona Rosenstein was Paul's Katherine Lowther.

The lunch bell rang and Paul went to the shed, where he took off his rubber boots and put on his torn canvas shoes. He went to the elevator and was pleased to find that it was running today.

He went down the eighteen floors to the marble lobby of the Sun Life Building. He went across the lobby and through the great brass doors, exchanging nods with the two officers of the Agricultural Police who always stood there.

It was a sunny day. He went down the broad granite steps into the street and across the street to Place Lévesque, which had once been called Dominion Square. He sat down on a bench, his paper bag beside him. But he had no appetite for lunch.

Again Mona filled his mind, and he tried to drive her out of it. He tried not to think of last night in the paint factory, when their naked bodies had been pressed together for one brief moment, her skin so soft and silky, making him so hot and hard and ready. He tried not to think of what ought to have happened next, the ultimate bliss they had never been able to experience together. Now, in London, perhaps she and Kevin would experience that bliss every night, several times a night. Paul had never known a thought more agonizing than this.

The only way to forget her would be to bury himself in the work that had to be done – political work. Already there were rival factions within the A.L.A. – hard-liners like Guido and a more liberal element composed of people like Paul. Paul would have to throw himself into that struggle to make sure that the right philosophy would prevail.

The hard-liners wanted to call it Angloland and the liberals wanted to call it New Canada. But there was much more to it than that; there was a basic difference of opinion about how to treat the French-speaking minority that would live within the boundaries of the new country.

The way a country treated its minorities, Paul believed, was a measure of whether a country was civilized or not. The rednecks in the A.L.A. wanted their Angloland to have English as its only official language. But that was all wrong, Paul felt. The country had to be fully and vigorously bilingual. Otherwise it would be just as repressive as Quebec, just as un-free, and nothing was more important than freedom.

Again Paul thought of Wolfe at Quebec, before dawn on that September morning of 1759. As the British soldiers sat in their boats, in the darkness, waiting to leap ashore and scale the impossible cliffs, a French sentry called out: "*Qui vive?*" Without hesitation, Captain Donald MacDonald, of the 78th Highlanders, answered: "*Convoi de vivres. Ne fais pas de bruit. Les Anglais nous entendront.*"

British bilingualism carried the day in 1759. Anglos must always remember to be bilingual. Unilingualism always meant defeat in this part of the world. President Chartrand was starting to learn that.

"Hi, Paul."

Paul looked up. It was Chucky.

"Hi, Chucky."

Chucky sat down on the bench, opened his brown paper bag, and took out the lunch his landlady had prepared.

"Well," Chucky said, "it was quite a weekend, wasn't it?"

"It sure was," said Paul.

Chucky bit into his delicious-looking roast beef sandwich. The sight of this made Paul hungry. From his paper bag he took out his own sandwich, which was made of the dry and crumbly leftovers of last night's supper, when Mrs. MacVicar had served something she called Mystery Meat Loaf.

225

NOV